HEALING YOUR INNER CHILD

HEALING YOUR INNER CHILD

© **Copyright 2024 - All rights reserved.**

Published 2024 by Sofia Visconti

The content contained within this book may not be reproduced, duplicated, or transmitted without direct written permission from the author or the publisher.

Under no circumstances will any blame or legal responsibility be held against the publisher, or author, for any damages, reparation, or monetary loss due to the information contained within this book, either directly or indirectly.

LEGAL NOTICE:

This book is copyright protected. It is only for personal use. You cannot amend, distribute, sell, use, quote, or paraphrase any part, or the content within this book, without the consent of the author or publisher.

DISCLAIMER NOTICE:

Please note the information contained within this document is for educational and entertainment purposes only. All effort has been executed to present accurate, up-to-date, reliable, complete information. No warranties of any kind are declared or implied. Readers acknowledge that the author is not engaged in the rendering of legal, financial, medical, or professional advice. The content within this book has been derived from various sources. Please consult a licensed professional before attempting any techniques outlined in this book.

By reading this document, the reader agrees that under no circumstances is the author responsible for any losses, direct or indirect, that are incurred as a result of the use of the information contained within this document, including, but not limited to, errors, omissions, or inaccuracies.

CLICK HERE

CONTENTS

INTRODUCTION 1

CHAPTER 1: RECOGNIZING AND UNDERSTANDING THE WOUNDED INNER... 12

HOW AN UNHEALED INNER CHILD FEELS 16
THINGS THAT CAUSED YOU TO FEEL UNSAFE IN YOUR CHILDHOOD 18
SIGNS YOU MIGHT STILL HAVE A WOUNDED INNER CHILD AS AN ADULT 21
THE SCIENCE OF TRAUMA: HOW CHILDHOOD TRAUMA AFFECTS YOUR BRAIN AND BEHAVIOR 28
   Heightened Stress Hormone Levels 28
   Epigenetics 30
   Impact on the Immune System 31
   Neurological Alterations 32
PERSONAL NARRATIVES: DEVELOPING INSECURE ATTACHMENT STYLES 33
   Anxious-Preoccupied 35
   Dismissive-Avoidant 35
   Disorganized (Fearful-Avoidant) 36

CHAPTER 2: METHODS AND TECHNIQUES FOR HEALING 40

PRACTICAL EXERCISES TO HEAL FROM CHILDHOOD TRAUMA 45
   Become Grounded 46
   Travel Back to Your Past 46
   Pay Attention to the Physical Sensations Arising 47
   Be Emotionally Present for Yourself and Name Every Emotion You Sense 48
   Compassionately Acknowledge Your Emotions .. 48
   Get in Touch With Your Core Needs That Were

    Unmet *49*
    Let It All Out *49*
    Let the Pain Go *50*
  TECHNIQUES FOR HEALING TRAUMA 50
    Eye Movement Desensitization and Reprocessing (EMDR) *50*
    Cognitive Processing Therapy (CPT) *51*
    Art or Music Therapy *51*
    Exposure Therapy *52*
  BREAKING HABIT LOOPS 52
    A Cue *53*
    Your Routine *53*
    Rewards..*53*
  EMBRACING SELF-LOVE AND SELF-COMPASSION 55

CHAPTER 3: PROCESSING THE PAIN AND FINDING PEACE... 62

  UNDERSTANDING THE LINK BETWEEN YOUR PAST AND PRESENT LIFE 64
  UNDERSTANDING DIFFERENT ATTACHMENT STYLES AND HOW THEY DEVELOP..70
  HOW TO HEAL AND DEVELOP A SECURE ATTACHMENT STYLE... 75
    Signs of Anxiously Preoccupied Attachment Style: *78*
    Signs of Dismissive Avoidant Attachment Style: 78
    Signs of Disorganized Fearful Avoidant Attachment Style:... *80*
    Signs of Secure Attachment Style: *81*
  HEALING STRATEGIES 82
    Step 1: Acceptance..*82*
    Step 2: Forgiveness *83*
    Step 3: Visualize Your New Life *85*
    Step 4: Action Out Your Plan *88*
    Step 5: Develop and Nurture a Strong Support

Network *92*
Step 6: Practice Mindful Living *94*
Step 7: Let Go of All Limitations *95*
Step 8: Enjoy Your New Life and Be Grateful *95*

CHAPTER 4: LIVING MINDFULLY AND LEARNING TO LOVE YOURSELF FULLY 98

DEVELOPING EMOTIONAL AWARENESS 101
Acknowledging Your Inner Child Feelings *102*
Meditate and Journaling *106*
Inject Playfulness Into Your Life *108*
Learn About Emotional Intelligence *109*
PRACTICE SETTING AND KEEPING HEALTHY BOUNDARIES 114
Uproot Unhealthy Limiting Beliefs and Build Empowering and Positive Beliefs *116*
Set New Values for Yourself *117*
Don't Dim Your Light to Make Others Comfortable *119*

CHAPTER 5: BUILDING HEALTHY RELATIONSHIP 122

NURTURING SELF-LOVE 125
Refrain From Comparing Yourself to Others *127*
Begin to Value Your Opinion of Yourself More . *128*
Accept That You Can't Make Everyone Happy . *129*
Permit Yourself to Make Mistakes *130*
Your Body Image Does Not Define Your Worth .*131*
Don't Accept Toxicity From People *132*
Face Your Fears *132*
Seize and Create Opportunities for Success *134*
You Should Always Come First *135*
Practice Bravery and Boldness *136*
Appreciate the Beauty Around You *137*
Make Kindness One of Your Core Values *138*

Celebrate Yourself Often *138*
CREATIVE IDEAS FOR BUILDING AND MAINTAINING
GREAT RELATIONSHIPS 139
  Mutual Support *139*
  Mature Conflict Management *140*
  Respect *140*
  Have Balance *141*
  Make Honesty Your Policy *142*
  Express Affection *142*
  Support Each Other's Vulnerabilities *143*
  Be Fun and Spontaneous *143*
  Accept Each Other's Differences *144*
  Work on Effective Communication *144*
  Practice Self-Regulation *145*
  Travel Together *145*
  Give Each Other Constructive Feedback *146*
  Empathy *146*
  Shared Goals *147*
  Small Thoughtful Gestures *148*
  Grow Together *148*

CHAPTER 6: FOSTERING LASTING HOLISTIC PERSONAL GROWTH 152

FINANCIAL GROWTH STRATEGIES 154
  Diversifying Income Streams *155*
  Open a Savings Account and Pay Yourself First *155*
  Budget and Stick To What You Planned *155*
  Invest for Your Retirement Funds *156*
  Don't Take High-Interest Loans *157*
  Pay Your Expenses on Time *157*
  Continue to Invest in Financial Education *157*
  Look After Yourself *158*
ACHIEVING A HEALTHY LIFESTYLE 158
  Let Go of Ultra-Processed Meals and Sugar *158*
  Sleep Hygiene *159*

Take Care of Your Gut *160*
Avoid Substance Abuse *161*
Become Friends With Spices and Herbs *161*
Meditation and Journaling *161*
ACHIEVING SOCIAL SUCCESS... 162
Research Places to Visit *163*
Treat Yourself Well *163*
Talk to People You Don't Know *163*
Join a Social Club *164*
Meet Up With Online Friends *164*
Plan to Meet Up With Old Friends *164*
Work on Your Active Listening Skills *165*
Give Genuine Compliments *165*
Spread Kindness *166*
Be More Approachable *166*
Overcome Your Insecurities *167*
Invest in Yourself *167*
Get What's Important Done First *168*
Forgive *168*
Support Your Friends and Family Members *169*
Find Ways to Make People Smile *169*
Challenge Yourself *170*

CONCLUSION **173**

REFERENCES **177**

INTRODUCTION

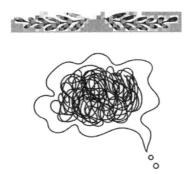

Have you ever sat down at night, struggling to sleep, wondering about the same questions over and over again? *Why do l keep repeating the same relationship patterns? Why do l keep attracting the same type of people? Why am I so afraid of life? Why is it so hard for me to be my authentic self? Why do l self-sabotage and play small? Where is my voice? Why am I so afraid to express myself? Where do all my feelings of insistent stress and anxiety come from? Why do I feel so drained? Why do I feel disconnected from my emotions? Why do I feel like a spectator in my own life? Is it even possible to be free from all my fears? Will I ever be comfortable in my skin and know who I really am? When is all this going to stop? How do I stop this vicious cycle of repeating negative experiences?*

If such questions and more like these haunts

you repeatedly, please do know that you aren't alone. We live in a broken world where certain unhealthy and abnormal patterns are normalized. We live in a world where many people find it easier to hate or hurt others while loving and being kind to the other person almost feels like a foreign concept. It's sad. When you grow up dehumanized, neglected, abused, bullied, belittled, and treated like you aren't worthy of love, care, and respect, all that becomes all you know. Unless someone ventures on a serious journey of healing and personal growth, they will repeat the same unkind things to their loved ones and children. Indeed, it is true that "hurt people really do hurt other people."

When we think of childhood trauma, it's easy to fall into the trap of blaming our parents or caregivers for not giving us the love and care we deeply need. However, things aren't always as simple as that. While it's true that other people knowingly just mistreat others, it's also true that sometimes the way parents bring up their children is merely a by-product or replication of how they were brought up. So, if they are not treated well, their emotions are invalidated constantly, and their needs are ignored, they are likely also to use the same parenting strategies on their children unless they are self-aware and developed.

Them hurting their children just because they possibly didn't know better doesn't negate how hurtful it is to raise one's child in a toxic way. Thus, all the feelings of children who grow up abused or mistreated are supposed to be validated no matter what. Even more, when they become adults, it's important to recognize that the pain of childhood trauma is deep and doesn't just go away simply because now you've aged. That pain continues to stay in our minds, hearts, and bodies until we fully do the inner child healing work. Unfortunately, it's impossible to stop attracting more pain and toxic experiences unless the work is done.

It's true that for many people, it wasn't their fault for experiencing the trauma or abuse they faced. However, what's important is to recognize that it's your responsibility to heal and break your connection to every negative cycle or pattern. You might feel like it's impossible to ever be okay again, but nothing could be any further from the truth. Change is possible! Human beings are designed with the unique ability to adapt and grow. Every day, thousands of cells in your body are working full time to replace dead cells with new cells and keep the healthy cells active and in good condition. Every time you learn something new or practice repeatedly new hobbies, your brain develops neural connections and gets reprogrammed 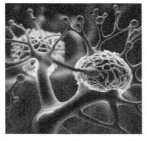 through a process called *neuroplasticity*. No matter what happened in your past, change is inevitable if you make up your mind to reclaim your true identity and life. Our past can only haunt and control us for as long as we allow it to. Once you decide that enough is enough, there is no limit to the amount of greatness that awaits you.

When you were young, your spirit was trampled upon and hurt multiple times. That child's soul may have been crushed and their voice silenced. In a bid to try to survive and not be cut off or abandoned by their caregivers, that child probably shed off parts of themselves and developed people-pleasing habits or coping mechanisms. All such survival strategies robbed the child of healthily living their life and developing a healthy relationship with themself. It's hard to love yourself when your environment keeps echoing to you the message that you aren't good enough unless you wear the masks people would rather see. It's hard to create healthy relationships with others when your self-worth is low. People can feel how we feel about ourselves. If someone detects that you don't love or value yourself, they are likely to poke at those insecurities and treat you poorly unless they are mature. This phenomenon explains why people who have unhealed childhood trauma often attract toxic relationships. Thus, if you have ever experienced toxic relationships, don't ever believe that that's all you are worthy of having. You deserve so much more. You are more than what your adverse childhood experiences forced you to believe about yourself.

When you experience trauma, your self-concept and self-worth are not the only things that change. Your brain also changes. That's why transformation has to also include the healing and growth of your brain. Your mind might have trained you to believe that there is danger and then feel afraid and want to run; that's where you now have to retrain the brain to teach it to see opportunities instead of threats everywhere. When you are an adult, you are no longer a helpless, dependent child who can't take responsibility for themself. Thus, it might have been understandable to have adopted certain coping mechanisms when you were a child, but once you grow older, you no longer need those things to protect you. There are many healthy ways you can protect and care for yourself. That's what this book is going to help you master. You will be equipped with tools to help you function at your best in your life. You will be able to learn to love yourself and others fearlessly and authentically.

Trauma changes the way you view yourself, others, and life. Through the lessons in this book, you will master how to regulate, think, behave, and perceive things correctly. Here are some myriad problems associated with experiencing childhood trauma (Aletheia, 2023):

- Struggling to set and maintain healthy boundaries.
- Being confused or unsure about your identity.
- A tendency to be a people-pleaser is seen as constantly abandoning your needs while catering to others.
- Being stagnant and unable to achieve your potential.
- Negative self-talk and being overly critical of oneself and others.
- Inability to regulate your emotions healthily. For example, often experience bouts of anger or suppress your emotions due to fear of rejection.

- Challenges with growing healthy and lasting relationships.
- Self-sabotage across every domain of your life. For example, in relationships, your health, or your health.
- Impulsive reactions.
- Disassociation or frequently checking out. Finding it hard to be present and grounded in reality.
- Low self-worth, self-esteem, self-confidence and often feeling inept.
- Have flashbacks or nightmares of the abuse, distress, or neglect you went through.
- Deteriorating physical health. For example, having insistent migraines and autoimmune diseases.
- Insecure attachment styles like dismissive-avoidant, fearful-avoidant, and anxious attachment.

This book will give you practical guidelines and tips on ways to make amends with the past and heal. You will finally be able to resolve your childhood trauma and be a healthy, securely attached individual. You will learn therapeutic techniques to resolve the trauma. These also include emotional regulation tools and cognitive behavioral therapy strategies. The inability to effectively communicate and set boundaries is a severe weakness that often leads to repeated cycles of toxic relationships. Hence, you will also be equipped with tools to reframe your self-image, build healthy self-esteem, and establish firm boundaries.

There is no way things will continue to be the same if you start to do things differently. Sometimes, when things don't go well, we may tend to focus on waiting for others to change, especially the people who hurt us. However, this is often futile since people only change when they want, not because you want them to. However, what you have control over is yourself. You can work on yourself and become who you have always wanted to be. This, in turn, inevitably allows you to attract a different reality that matches your frequency, vibration, and who you would have evolved to become.

Your inner child is more than just a common

metaphor used in psychology. It represents you and the experiences you went through. Your inner child is the key to understanding who you are as an adult and why certain things often transpire the way they do, specifically in your life. This book offers you a holistic approach to healing, manifesting a fulfilling life full of abandonment and positive experiences. Your mental health deserves your love and care. You deserve to be who you were meant to be and achieve the life of your dreams. You are more than enough and worthy of happiness and freedom from your pain. Are you ready to get started? Let's dive in!

CHAPTER 1
RECOGNIZING AND UNDERSTANDING THE WOUNDED INNER CHILD IN YOU

Being a parent does not only entail physically looking after your child. It also involves being there for them psychologically, emotionally, mentally, and spiritually. It's understanding and accepting that a child is helpless at a certain stage. They wholly depend on you to keep them holistically safe in a world that's all new to them. Sadly, this is not always something every parent understands before they start a family. Therefore, what ends up taking place is the child growing up in a dysfunctional and unsafe environment. They cry and signal for help, but those bids for attention are ignored or outrightly dismissed. The child learns that they can't rely on their caregivers for support. As a result, many problems start to unfold as the child tries to adapt to different coping mechanisms to survive. This is what gives rise to childhood trauma and wounds.

Although the adults meant to look after children should ideally fulfill their role well, it's also important to make room for empathy and understand why some caregivers might struggle to fulfill their responsibilities. The pain inflicted on the child is usually, in most cases, unintentional. Most times the caregivers might actually be oblivious to what's happening and the impact of their parenting style on the child's overall development. Some adults just continue to generational traumas by treating their children the same way they were treated. This often happens if the parents came from an unsafe background and didn't end up taking responsibility for their healing when they grew up. As a result, how they treat their children is all that they know. That's the only way they know how to love and care for others. That's the blueprint their caregivers passed on to them. Unless they are open to change and growth, they, too, become limited to what's familiar to them, even though it might be toxic parenting styles.

Having reviewed these possible reasons why caregivers treat children the way they do, it's important to consider forgiving them for their inability to give you what you need. For most people, if they had known better, they probably would have treated you better and given you a healthy childhood experience. When we don't look at things this way, we run the risk of living the rest of our lives bitter and in victim mode, always blaming others for what they didn't give us instead of taking control and being responsible for our healing now that we are grown.

Now, let's revisit the past. Childhood wounds start to appear when a child feels endangered. These wounds are deep-seated and emotional. They affect the child's psyche and even impair their brain development. The child starts to grow up seeing the world from a very different outlook. Instead of life and the world being an exciting adventure to explore and enjoy, almost everything feels frightening and dangerous. The child starts to grow up with a heightened fight and flee-activated nervous system. Instead of being relaxed and having a positive view of themselves, they grow up and start to live on edge and feel defective.

The underlying core belief most people who have Childhood trauma have is that "There is something wrong with me; that's why people don't love me or care about my needs and feelings." This core belief is what breaks down the child's self-worth and self-esteem and shatters their confidence. It makes the child fearful of social interactions or relationships. They start to believe that since their closest people abandoned them, they will never be lovable and accepted by anyone else. To learn more about the effects of childhood trauma and how to identify the wounds or recognize the impact of it, let's move on to the next section.

How an Unhealed Inner Child Feels

Your inner child is a part of who you are, the child you are that lives inside your psyche. No matter how much we age, our inner child never dies. That child represents how you felt or saw the world when you were young. That  child carries the memories of all that happened to you in your past. That child might either be happy, sad, or numb. The well-being of that child will determine your well-being and overall happiness. If that child still has unresolved wounds and pain, they won't stop hurting until that pain is addressed. Whenever that child is hurting, you are also hurting. Whenever that child is healed, you are also healed, and the outcome of your life experiences gives a testament to what's going on within you. People who are hurting or tend to hurt others signify that they have an unhealed inner child that's crying out for comfort, love, safety, and healing. Unless that child is healed, there is no end to the cycle of problems that will keep coming because of unresolved past trauma.

We must stay connected to our inner child because they are part of who we are. When we numb that child's feelings and silence their voice, pain is inevitable. It's important to know the primary condition of your inner child. For adults who grew up with childhood trauma, that inner child probably feels this way most of the time:

- Very afraid of the world and people.
- Plagued with insistent feelings of inadequacy and worthlessness.
- Strongly believe they are unlovable.
- Struggles to trust people.
- Has constant negative self-talk.
- May think positively of others but negatively of oneself.
- Feels like a burden to others and may want to isolate or be hyper-independent as a result of this belief.
- Thinks they are not smart or gifted.

- Feels ashamed of who they are.
- Believes they are defective and not worthy of love, care, and respect.
- Struggles with self-doubt.
- Has low self-esteem.
- Feels insecure and often self-conscious.
- Believes they deserve to be punished or ill-treated.
- Believes they are not a good person.
- Always self-critical.
- Doesn't feel safe.
- Undermines their strengths and overinflates their weaknesses.

This is not even an exhaustive list. All these feelings are pervasive no matter where you go or what age you are unless healing takes place. When your inner child still feels this way, it means that's how you feel about yourself at the core of your being. Your life becomes a reflection of these ingrained beliefs and feelings. The question is, what really causes this painful and harmful way of viewing yourself and others? Let's find out the answers in the next section.

Things That Caused You to Feel Unsafe in Your Childhood

Do you recall how your caregivers responded to you when you were young? When you expressed distress and reached out for help, what were the typical responses you would get?

Below are common patterns you would notice from a child who was raised without adequate emotional attunement and experienced neglect on different levels (Merck, 2018):

- Having your ideas or opinions was shunned. You were forced to only go along with what was presented to you. This leads you to lose confidence in your thoughts or capabilities.
- When you express yourself authentically, you would either be punished or scolded.
- Being spontaneous and free was discouraged. You had to follow rigid rules and ways to live or do things.
- Spending time with friends, exploring your interests, or just doing what you wanted was not allowed.

- Showing negative feelings or emotions was not allowed. If you tried to express your discomfort or hurt, you would be accused of being ungrateful or selfish.
- You would be laughed at, humiliated, looked down upon, and shamed for who you are by your family members.
- Thoughtless words were often hurled at you, and you were expected to just take it. It became "normal" to accept verbal and emotional abuse.
- You were violated physically either by being beaten down or screamed at, pushed around, or your physical possessions like clothes or toys taken without your permission.
- Your caregivers made you feel responsible for their needs and happiness. They blamed you for their problems and made it an expectation for you to do something about it.
- You weren't allowed to focus on your needs. Doing this would lead to being accused of being selfish or bad.
- Physical affection or words of affirmation were rare. You would constantly be criticized, and almost all the good things you did would be downplayed.

- People would lie about you to always get you in trouble and find justifications for scapegoating you.
- It was rare to experience any form of emotional attunement or support. You had to learn to soothe yourself and be self-reliant.
- You were left to figure out life or deal with your pain alone.
- When people were nice to you, it was usually only when you took on the people-pleasing role. Unconditional love was almost nonexistent. Love was almost like a transaction you had to complete. If your parents are nice to you, then it would mean you had to either abandon yourself and focus on doing whatever they wanted or suffer the consequences of negligence if you didn't comply.

Constantly going through such experiences was probably what you went through for most of your childhood. This would mean that your inner child largely felt alone, misunderstood, unloved, unaccepted, judged, criticized, engulfed, and neglected for the most part.

Signs You Might Still Have a Wounded Inner Child as an Adult

We don't just simply get over our past just

because we want to. The pain of what happened had to be processed first. Suppressing those

memories and emotions only prolongs the suffering. One way or the other, the wounded child will still leave a trail of tears across every aspect of your life until that child's pain is validated, and they are given a chance to experience what they always needed. This means that in our adult lives, or even as you were growing up, chances are that you started experiencing the aftereffects of having a broken childhood. Let's now review what some signs of a wounded inner child are that you might experience:

- You feel like you must always be responsible for other people's problems and happiness, especially those close to you or family members.
- You often deny your authentic reality and operate in "people-pleaser mode."
- You are an error hoarder. You don't easily let go, express your hurt, and forgive. You internalize your hurt instead of acting out in passive-aggressive ways.

- You can stand up for others but find it hard to stand up for yourself. People often walk over you and see you as weak.
- You struggle to be assertive, articulate yourself, or think on the spot. When someone attacks you, instead of thinking on your feet an assertive response to give them, you either freeze or just let them treat you anyhow.
- You always feel inadequate and not good enough. This makes you downplay your abilities and settle for less.
- You often find yourself in relationships with toxic or abusive patterns.
- You believe that you are, deep down, a really bad person. No matter what you do, you feel like everyone can still see how defective or bad you are.
- You feel like people are ashamed of associating with you, so at times, or most times, you isolate yourself due to this belief.
- You often feel uncomfortable in your own skin and appear rigid to others.
- You are very hard on yourself and expect perfection. This attitude may also spill onto others as you tend to reject them when they are imperfect, just like how

you were rejected as a child for not being perfect.
- You lack confidence and self-efficacy. As a result, you have trouble getting certain things done from start to finish. You tend to easily write yourself off.
- You over-give and over-function in relationships. This may be due to the belief that you are not worthy of love for just who you are.
- You might have a type A personality or show signs of being an overachiever. This comes from an unhealthy place whereby you believe that anything less than perfect will cause you to not be loved or accepted by others. So, you don't take failure very well.
- You have trouble having a growth mindset. You tend to be fixed and set in your ways because you don't easily believe in your ability to change. You also fear trying new things due to the fear of failure and rejection.
- You feel like you don't belong.
- You often find yourself feeling misunderstood by others and in constant fights.
- You struggle with so much anxiety.

- You desire love, connection, and intimacy but can sometimes push away people when they come too close. This happens because subconsciously, you have learned to associate "love" with pain since your caregivers who were meant to love you caused you so much pain and suffering.

- You don't trust anyone, including yourself.
- You feel very isolated in your life. Most of your relationships tend to be surface level.
- You often find yourself chasing people to love you or having unrequited love instead of mutual love and respect.

- You have an intense fear of people and tend to avoid social interactions as much as possible.
- You might have some form of addiction that you use to numb your pain or run away from it. This could be being a workaholic, alcoholic, drug addict, sex addict, binge eater, or tending to watch pornography a lot.
- You struggle to be interdependent; you are either hyper-independent or too dependent on others.
- You might have anger management issues or passive-aggressive behavior.
- You tend to attract unhealthy partners like users, abusers, narcissists, or other people with insecure attachment styles.
- You might have a pattern of mistreating the people close to you. Without realizing it, the way you were treated by your caregivers might be the same way you start to treat others.
- You might be codependent and struggle with self-love deficiency.
- You often neglect yourself. Self-care and meeting your needs might be difficult for you. You may even feel bad for doing something nice for yourself.

- You might have an urge to rebel or retaliate in some way. In extreme cases, you might find yourself indulging in criminal activities and detached from other people's feelings.
- You may struggle to have empathy for others since you never got to experience empathy in your childhood.
- You struggle to understand yourself. Self-reflection might not always be an easy thing for you to do. Since you already believe that you are a bad person, the last thing you may want is to always have that thrown in your face or think about it. This is also why you may have a habit of avoiding difficult conversations and being defensive.
- You feel safe alone. Even though you crave connection, you may also have a strong desire to be left alone most times due to your alone time feeling like that's the only time you will ever be safe from the "harsh world out there."
- You struggle to know who you really are. Identity crisis is a common theme in your life.
- You often look for external validation to feel good about yourself.

The Science of Trauma: How Childhood Trauma Affects Your Brain and Behavior

Experiencing an adverse childhood doesn't only hurt the child's emotions. It also causes serious damage to their brain and negatively affects their personality development.

Below are some examples of how childhood trauma causes severe brain damage.

Heightened Stress Hormone Levels

Cortisol and adrenaline are stress hormones often released whenever there is any sort of perceived or real threats and danger. However, when these hormones are released and prompt you to take action, they cause  your blood to flow to different parts of your body except the "thinking part" of the brain. This basically means that when your stress hormone levels are high, you switch to survival mode, and reason and rationality often get thrown out the window.

For example, if you think that someone wants to hurt you, you may not have the capacity to even question the rationality of your thought and just quickly act in a way to protect yourself from that person. As a result, if that person wanted to be your friend but you interpreted their closeness as a threat, you end up pushing them away one way or the other.

Bear in mind that all this may just be in your head. Reality might be totally different. They just wanted to be your friend, but because your stress hormone levels are often high, you just end up acting out of fear and being prone to negative bias. When such experiences get repeated over someone's social experiences, it can lead to *social thinning*. This is whereby people also start to reject or walk away from you since you reject or think the worst of them. Experiencing this outcome also ends up leading to more repeated traumatic events as you start to feel like people always reject you and assume that it's really because you are defective or unlovable. It's highly unlikely that you will realize that your outlook on life and response to things is what's actually causing the negative cycles to repeat themselves. This correct perception of reality can only come a little through self-awareness and healing work.

It's unhealthy for the body to keep operating under high-stress levels. Physically, if it continues, you may begin to be at risk for struggling with high blood pressure and high blood glucose levels—which may result in type diabetes later on in life, abdominal obesity, development of lupus, poor immune system, osteoporosis, and a myriad of mental health problems such as depression (Merck, 2018).

When hormone levels change in irregular and radical ways, it eventually affects the overall infrastructure of the brain and possibly causes lifelong health problems.

Epigenetics

Have you ever heard of the phrase "gene modification?" This is basically when your genes change or get turned off or on depending on your life experiences and the environment you live in. The study of how genes alter is called epigenetics. For instance, you may have grown up being multi-talented, but due to being talked down or mistreated, you might end up being able to do only a few things, which might not be even a quarter of your true innate potential. Or if you were born with the capacity to be free-spirited and fearless, abuse and childhood trauma can instill fear in you to the point where it becomes who you are.

Trauma causes gene modification. It can stifle your growth and abilities and even affect your physical features. Have you ever noticed people who used to look very different from how they ended up looking when their lives changed for the better? Maybe they didn't have outstanding physical features deemed by society as being "good-looking." But suddenly, the moment poverty and hardship go out the window, they evolve and look like a totally different person, stunning from head to toe. That's the bright side of epigenetics! The sad part is that child abuse and trauma can make someone's physical features not very pleasant or make them have stunted growth.

Impact on the Immune System

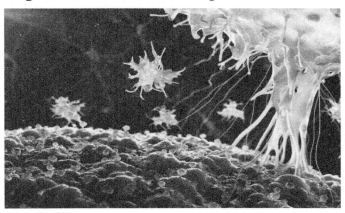

Your brain also controls the immune system. Your immune system is inevitably affected if your brain isn't healthy. Your immune system is a network of cells, nerves, organs, and tissues all working together to protect your body and serve you. You are shielded from diseases, and your cells renew and grow because of your immune system.

When someone experiences trauma, their immunity is impaired or compromised due to irregular and abnormal hormonal level fluctuations. You are also likely to experience inflammation very easily and take longer to heal from diseases compared to a healthy person with a normal upbringing.

Examples of diseases associated with having impaired immunity include asthma, allergies, anxiety, cardiovascular disease, depression, and being at risk of getting cancer too.

Neurological Alterations

Our brains are made up of billions of neurons that control our ability to learn, see, hear, reason, and form neural pathways for the habits we have.

When those neurons are exposed to high levels of stress hormones, it can weaken them and prevent them from being able to do their job well. This means that you may end up growing up with memory retention problems, learning disorders, difficulty coping with stress, and overall restrained cognitive ability. If that child had the potential to be an A student at school, they might end up just scoring average or even worse marks due to how their brain was affected adversely.

They might also become so used to the negative habits they adopted as a way to survive, such as being alone most of the time and having extreme social anxiety due to the way their neural pathways developed to reinforce those new coping mechanisms. For instance, you might have an avoidant attachment style and assume that that's just how you are; you prefer to be a loner. However, that might not actually be a true reflection of how you originally would have been if you weren't exposed to childhood trauma. Your personality might just be what your brain adjusted to thinking, and that's how it can protect you from "danger."

Personal Narratives: Developing Insecure Attachment Styles

Most people who have childhood trauma end up with an insecure attachment style. However, this can be changed, and someone can become securely attached once they heal. The attachment theory was developed by a psychologist called John Bowlby in the 1950s. This was after he experimented and observed how babies reacted to their mothers under different conditions.

Your attachment style is how you relate and bond to people based on your perception of social interactions or people. This style is formed during childhood based on how your caregivers respond to your needs.

There are three insecure attachment styles, namely (Moore, 2022):

- Anxious-preoccupied
- Avoidant-dismissive
- Disorganized (fearful-avoidant)

A child who has healthy development ends up growing up with a secure attachment style. This happens when the caregivers are responsive to their child's needs, loving, and emotionally attuned, not only sporadically but consistently.

This makes the child grow up trusting people and feeling worthy of love and care. They also become brave enough to explore the world, try new things, and play because they know that if they cry out for help, their caregivers will show up. This becomes the blueprint for their relationships growing up. Let's explore insecure attachment styles more.

Anxious-Preoccupied

This insecure attachment style usually develops within the first 18 months of a child's life. During this formative stage, the child gets inconsistent attention and attunement from their caregivers. One moment they might be loving and present; the next, they are distant or just negligent.

The child may start to interpret that inconsistency very negatively and feel like their caregiver is unpredictable and unreliable. So even when the caregiver is there, the child might still be on edge and untrusting because they think they will be left in no time again. The child grows up longing for love and always feeling like they have to please their parents just to avoid abandonment. This can also go on in adult relationships where you see anxiously attached people always chasing love, abandoning their needs while pleasing their partners just to get their validation, presence, and love.

Dismissive-Avoidant

This style develops when the caregivers are very emotionally neglectful and insensitive to the child's needs. The child might have gone to the parent expressing discomfort or crying and then forced to be quiet or not show any negative emotion. This would then force the child to always resort to self-soothing strategies and grow up hyper-independent.

In adult relationships, dismissive avoidants continue the same pattern of being overly self-reliant, dismissing their emotions and other people's emotions, or believing that they are defective. This comes from interpreting their rejection in childhood as a sign of disapproval or that something is wrong with them. So, they grow up with shame and fear of intimacy even though they need it the most. They avoid people or maintain surface-level relationships because they fear that if people get close, they will see how defective they are and leave them.

Disorganized (Fearful-Avoidant)

Children who experience child abuse or grow up in bizarre and dysfunctional families often end up developing this attachment style. The caregivers raise the child in unpredictable ways. One moment, they are loving, and the next, they are being aggressive or outright abusive to the child.

A child might be punished for something, and then rewarded for the same thing at other times. So, the child ends up confused and fearful in their relationships. They form the belief that people close to you are not always safe. Hence, they often tend to run away from people and also come back because they know the flip side of how someone can be.

Fearful-avoidant adults can end up being in relationships where the same childhood trauma they experienced is replicated. If unhealed, they can unfortunately and unintentionally also treat their children the same way. Hence perpetuating the cycle of generational trauma and abuse.

The good news in all this is that even though you might have grown up experiencing adverse and traumatic things, it's possible to heal and develop a secure attachment style. That's the beauty of the journey you are on now. The more you learn new ways of seeing yourself and the world, the better you become equipped to free yourself from past hurts and heal your inner child.

This chapter has explored the problem of childhood trauma and how its effects show up as time goes on. Let's move on to the next chapter, where we will explore techniques for healing and recreating healthy new beginnings.

CHAPTER 2
METHODS AND TECHNIQUES FOR HEALING

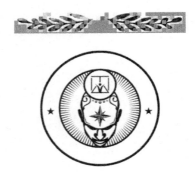

When we undergo childhood trauma, a lot of painful emotions are generated. Often, the child fails to have the support needed to process that trauma. Their caregivers might be distant and unable to attune to the child's emotional needs. This leaves the child feeling neglected and having to deal with heavy emotions that they don't even understand well. The easiest yet hurtful option to survive would be to either numb and suppress those emotions or just enmesh and morph yourself into whatever people want you to be like.

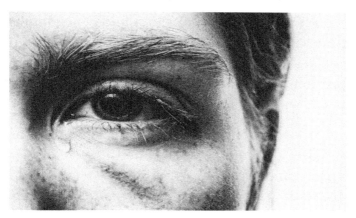

However, doing this doesn't make the trauma go away. Ignoring emotions doesn't make them disappear. They remain stored up as energy in our minds and bodies. Those emotions start to manifest in our lives either through passive-aggressive ways or addictive behaviors such as overreliance on drugs, substances, food, sex, and even being a workaholic and perfectionist. Your personality becomes largely influenced by your coping mechanisms. You lose the essence of who you truly are. You can even spend years of your life struggling with identity crises and the inability to connect deeply with others. Healing means taking time to address all that pain, process the emotions that weren't dealt with, and reframe your mindset so that you adopt the correct beliefs and thoughts about yourself and others.

True healing is a journey where you commit to connecting to the authentic version of who you are. You learn to embrace your emotions, be present for yourself and others, and meet your needs without feeling guilty for doing so.

Since most intense emotions like anger or sadness are often shamed or socially unacceptable, you might struggle to face them and even feel like what's the point. However, you now have to give yourself the attunement and presence you always longed to receive from your caregivers. Refusal to accept the difficult emotions within you only makes healing impossible because you would be disassociating from your pain.

Perhaps you might have grown up being

scolded whenever you showed pain or cried. Your parents might have said to you, "Stop crying," and dismissed your pain when you needed their empathy and understanding the most. This may make you grow up believing that it's wrong to feel your emotions. However, nothing could be any further from the truth. Once emotions are felt and processed, they pass away like clouds fade away. However, not dealing with them is similar to clouds getting bigger and heavier and yet not raining. Feeling and processing your emotions is like seeing clouds finally release the rain. It will only rain for a few hours, days, weeks, or months, but the rain will gradually stop. Similarly, healing will

be difficult, and you will feel those emotions for a while, but eventually, things will clear up. You inevitably reach a place of emotional and mental clarity. This frees you to invest more of your energy in building your life instead of worrying about unresolved hurt.

Before we dive into the methods of healing, let's unpack examples of the painful incidents that you might have gone through. Those experiences might include:

- Losing a loved one and not knowing how to process the grief.
- Being exposed to domestic violence.
- Going through emotional, verbal, sexual, or physical abuse.
- Experiencing racism.
- Lack of physical and emotional care. Not being given basic needs such as adequate food, a safe shelter, or clothing.
- Having your emotions constantly dismissed or shamed.
- Being bullied at school.
- Transactional love. You only got treated kindly whenever you did something for your caregivers, like tending to their needs or acting the way they wanted you to.
- Being left to care for yourself when you were sick.
- Frequently being passed around relatives and changing homes due to not having a stable long-term caregiver.
- Seeing adults under the influence of drugs and alcohol.
- Witnessing a parent being abused by their partner.
- Being forced to raise other children while you were also a child.

- Not being allowed to chase your dreams or have friends. Your life had to revolve around being available to do whatever your caregivers wanted.

Practical Exercises to Heal From Childhood Trauma

One of the biggest motivators for healing from childhood trauma is looking into the horizon and seeing how your future can turn out to be once you free yourself. Think about it: Up until now, most of your relationships and life choices might have been deeply damaged by the wounds you incurred from your past. You might have had a pattern of pushing away people, downplaying yourself, self-sabotaging, moving with low confidence, distrusting others, avoiding social interactions, self-inflicting pain on yourself, attracting toxic relationships, and so on. All of that can now become a thing of the past once you dive into the healing work. The main objective of healing from childhood trauma is to accept what happened and grow from it. It's to allow yourself to use your hardships as fuel for unleashing the best version of yourself instead of letting what happened consume and break you down. Ready to get started? Let's begin.

Become Grounded

Our minds are always racing to many places and filled with thoughts of the past, present, or future. To interrupt that pattern, take some time to become grounded in the present. Bring your full attention to the "now." Feel your spirit and soul reside inside your body. Be present inside your body. You can take time to feel the tension and weight your body is carrying. Massage yourself gently while you still train yourself to be fully in the moment.

Travel Back to Your Past

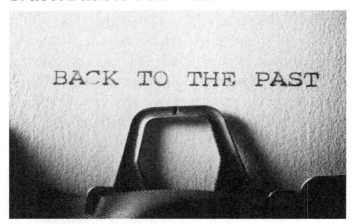

Once you have practiced being fully present with yourself, try your best to recall what usually triggers you. What are the things people say, do, think, or don't do that set you off? Which incidents triggered you the most? Why do you think they did? What do you think could be the underlying problem or pain point? Can you think of something in your past that created the wound you noticed? For example, if you have a pattern of easily giving up relationships or instantly blocking someone you feel violated your trust, could there possibly be someone in your past who did the same thing to you? Write down everything that comes to mind. Recall as much as you can and record everything that comes to your mind. Bear in mind that revisiting your past might evoke dormant emotions in you to hit you very hard. If this happens, don't run away. Continue to allow yourself to feel the pain and keep looking deeper into what happened.

Pay Attention to the Physical Sensations Arising

Once you start diving into the past, your mind might not be able to recognize that you are safe and not in danger like how you were when the events that hurt you happened. So, your fight-and-flee response is likely to be activated. This is your body also showing you how you probably felt when the traumatic events happened. You might sense tightness, notice your heart race more, and even start to sweat or feel lightheaded. All this is happening because your emotions are percolating. Take your time to explore all the sensations you are getting and label them as much as you can; for example, "I feel terrified and unsafe."

Be Emotionally Present for Yourself and Name Every Emotion You Sense

Printing a list of different names for emotions beforehand can help correctly identify and understand each emotion you notice. Try your best not to block out uncomfortable emotions. Instead, allow yourself to feel them and label each of them using "I" statements. For example, "I am deeply hurt and feel worthless." "I don't feel lovable because my parents always wanted me to be someone I'm not and didn't compliment who I am. I am angry at them for that."

Compassionately Acknowledge Your Emotions

For most of your life, your emotions might have been vilified and despised. Now it's time to acknowledge and compassionately accept them as part of who you are. Accept them as your loving messengers sent to inform you about your truth. Without them, you would be disconnected from the reality of the impact of what happened to you. Your emotions were there to advocate for you and be your voice. Start loving them more than ever before, all of them; this includes anger, bitterness, anything and everything! This exercise helps you to no longer be at war with yourself but learn to fight the real enemy—the injustice that happened to you.

Get in Touch With Your Core Needs That Were Unmet

Being in touch with your emotions, listening to them, feeling the pain, and processing everything helps you to notice what caused all the pain. You will start to have ideas of what you needed that you were deprived of. Write down everything that comes to  mind. Be very clear about your needs, because, to this day, you are still craving to have those needs met. Tell yourself that you deserve to have your needs met and begin to acknowledge each one of them instead of living in disassociation.

Let It All Out

Writing is a great way to give your emotions a voice. Let it all out. Share everything you recall. If you wish to speak to someone, you can do so. Let them know that you don't need advice or anything; you just want them to be present with you in your experiences. Also, write down all the counterproductive coping mechanisms you adopted in a bid to survive. Then, write how you would respond differently to those situations now that you know better and can protect yourself.

Let the Pain Go

After processing everything, it's now time to return to your body in the present and move forward on a clean slate. If there is someone you want to express your resentment or anger to, you can write a letter to that person, read it out loud, and burn it once you are done. Visualize all the energy and pain that was stored up inside you. If you get triggered again and experience a relapse, don't be hard on yourself. It just means that some wounds might need more time before you can fully be healed from their impact. You can repeat this process when necessary until you feel fully liberated from your past.

Techniques for Healing Trauma

When working with a therapist or someone else who can support your healing journey, these techniques can be very helpful in your path to overcoming past trauma.

Eye Movement Desensitization and Reprocessing (EMDR)

This is a psychotherapy approach to helping reduce the effects of trauma. It can lessen the intensity of memories you have of what happened before. It works by moving your eyes from side to side while also harnessing talk therapy to explore and reframe negative beliefs, thoughts, and emotions that were repressed in you. You can make use of affirmations to silence negative self-talk and reprogram your mind for healing and health.

Cognitive Processing Therapy (CPT)

This is an action-focused approach to healing the effects of childhood trauma. You do this by examining your life and taking note of negative cycles and patterns that resulted from the unhealthy beliefs and thoughts you adopted from experiencing trauma. You learn to adapt to new ways of approaching things. You start to practice thinking, talking, and acting differently. All this allows you to no longer be a victim of your past. It can also help you start to perform very well in your endeavors due to no longer having negative voices and the wrong outlook on life holding you back.

Art or Music Therapy

Sometimes, you might find it hard to express yourself through words. In such situations, using art and singing can help you to express yourself. You can use images and colors or the emotions in certain parts of your songs to tell your story.

Exposure Therapy

This is a very effective way to heal from the effects of trauma. Trauma makes us avoid things we are afraid of. For example, you might avoid socializing, confrontations, conflict, getting close to people, or being emotionally expressive. The only way you can heal from this is by doing the very thing you avoid. You can only heal from this by doing the very thing you avoid. This allows you to confront your fears and no longer allow them to run your life.

Breaking Habit Loops

If you've observed your habits closely before doing anything, there is always a loop that you follow. This loop is comprised of three components that trigger you to action out something. Let's review what those components are.

A Cue

Before doing something you often do, a cue or trigger usually makes you participate in your habits. This cue could be a specific place, time, emotional state, what you watch, or being around certain people. For example, if you lay on your bed during the day, you will likely take a nap or watch Netflix. In this case, being in bed is the cue that triggers the habit of napping or Netflix and chilling.

Your Routine

We all follow some pattern every day. Maybe you always wake up at 6:00 a.m. Or perhaps you enjoy snacking just before bedtime. You are likely to repeat most habits mainly because your mind has been programmed to repeat them at certain times.

Rewards

You will most likely repeat habits that you feel have the most benefits for you. For example, if you feel that sleeping helps you feel better, you will likely repeat that habit consistently. You would be less motivated to repeat habits that aren't pleasurable to you.

You can break your habit loop by identifying the habits that are pulling you back. So check your routine and decide to replace that time with a new habit that will yield better results for you. Be mindful of your triggers. Try to avoid places or things that make it hard for you to resist bad habits. For example, if you keep going to fast-food restaurants when yet you want to eat healthy, it might make that goal almost impossible to achieve. Another way to kick start new habits is to use your guilty pleasures as your reward. If you attach something exciting to look forward to once you finish a habit you find boring or addictive, you can have enough motivation to get it done.

Finally, the key to creating new habits is to consistently keep doing them until new neural pathways are formed in your brain that allow those habits to be repeated almost automatically or naturally without you having to force yourself so much. The same goes for overcoming bad behaviors we might have adopted due to childhood traumas. For instance, if you always keep people at arm's length, you can practice being more open to deep conversations and sharing your life with others. Don't isolate yourself. The more you keep at it, the less social anxiety you will have.

Embracing Self-Love and Self-Compassion

One of the biggest core wounds resulting from childhood trauma is self-love deficiency. Learning how to develop this love for ourselves is important instead of always looking for it outside us. No measure of love we get outside ourselves will ever be  enough to quench the thirst our soul has for self-love.

Below are some helpful tips to help you cultivate deep-seated compassion for yourself and lasting self-love:

- **Permit yourself to make mistakes:** You probably recall being hurt and rejected for making mistakes and consequently terrified of failure. However, life gives you countless growth opportunities where you won't always have answers to everything. Only leaping when you are sure you won't fail may stifle your growth and make it hard for you to feel self-actualized. Therefore, start to commit to being a risk taker. Remember that there is no such thing as failure if you try to improve yourself. Remember that no matter what happens, you will always be there to cheer for yourself. Embrace the growth mindset and remember that making mistakes is human!

- **Love yourself the way you would love someone you deeply care about:** It's often very easy to love others. We are, at times, willing to sacrifice so much for those we love and yet give ourselves breadcrumbs. Create a blueprint of how you would love someone you care about. Start doing all those things for you. Be emotionally available for yourself and start being sensitive and responsive to your needs.
- **Maintain healthy boundaries:** Before, you might have let others walk all over you. However, now it's time to learn to say no and only do what you deem best. It's okay to say no to your loved ones if they expect too much from you. It's okay to avoid toxic relationships and call out unacceptable behaviors. Start standing your ground and learning how to be more assertive.
- **Use affirmations to reframe your mindset:** Traumatic experiences can

incite a pattern of constant negative self-talk. You might have believed very negative things about yourself and others. Start to detox all that poison and replace unhealthy thoughts with empowering and positive affirmations. Connect to your true worth and practice showing up as the person you have always wanted to be.

- **Never compromise your self-care:** Take some time each day to look after your body, soul, and mind. Nourish your mind with books that grow your confidence and self-esteem. Take some time to exercise each day. Eat healthy. Sleep well. Make some time to connect with others and enjoy relationships. Continue to unleash your full potential.
- **Journal:** Write your thoughts and progress daily. Set goals and have clear action plans on what you will do to create the life of your dreams. Ask for help where need be. Nourish your connections and leverage your support network to help to improve.
- **Build your self-trust:** Develop a healthy relationship with yourself by committing to always keep your word. Once you set your mind on something, do

it. The more you accomplish your goals and get things done, the more your self-efficacy will grow. Your self-trust will improve, and this will give you momentum to keep taking on bigger challenges in life. Be clear about your purpose, and never stop at anything until you achieve it.

- **Forgive those who hurt you:** Holding on to resentment is like drinking poison and expecting people who hurt you to suffer. It's not worth it. It only makes you miserable and prevents you from being your best self to others. Begin to let go of all past hurts. If there are conversations you feel need to be had for you to have closure, reach out to the people and speak about it respectfully. Doing this can be the beginning of new, beautiful relationships with people who hurt you. Speak your truth and live your truth no matter what; authenticity is gold.

Now that we have covered methods you can employ to begin your healing journey let's move forward to unpacking more on what you can do to recreate the life you wish to see. The next chapter will explore ways to set effective boundaries, enhance emotional intelligence, and cultivate authentic relationships.

CHAPTER 3
PROCESSING THE PAIN AND FINDING PEACE

One of the most frustrating things is to know that something is not okay, but you just can't put a finger on it. We see ourselves repeating the same cycles of failed relationships, living with the same fears, sabotaging our success, and living way below our potential. Even though it can be evident that there is a huge problem that needs to be resolved, not knowing what that problem is exactly can make us postpone working on solving things. We start to give in to distractions and even lie to ourselves that we are happy.

However, the heart always knows its own pain and bitterness. While we are in our own company, our lives flash before us, and we get the same reminders that things are not okay. Sadness starts to sink into our hearts. Contentment and lasting joy become rare. No matter how much we achieve today, our unhealed past still haunts us until we gather the courage to face it. Not doing so means living the rest of our lives, lacking peace of mind, and settling for mediocrity. This chapter is meant to help you travel back to your past and make sense of it.

What really happened? Why did you end up having the personality you have now? Where does your deep-rooted sadness come from? Where do all your fears come from? Why do they have such a strong hold on you? Who is the real you? If it wasn't forgo-getters all the adverse childhood experiences you had, who would you have evolved to be? Do you remember who originally hurt you? What were the needs you had when you were a child that were either violated or neglected? What happened? Can you travel back with me now? You don't have to do it alone.

Understanding the Link Between Your Past and Present Life

At this stage, you have to get ready to face your past in its entirety. Get ready to sit in the true reality of what happened to you. It's the only way you can be emotionally detoxed and set free from the pain from your past that has been driving most of your decisions about how you choose to live.

Writing is one of the best ways to give yourself a safe outlet to pour out your heart. Find a quiet place without distractions where you can have a meditative state and listen to all the pain that you have been repressing for long. It's now time to give your inner child a voice. Let that child speak their truth and express everything. Do you notice how that child has been trying their best to be heard throughout your life up until now?

That child is the one who tells you that they don't feel safe in certain situations, and it would manifest as you choose to either isolate yourself from certain people and environments or just keep others at arm's length. That child still cries out for intimacy, though. This manifests in your chasing after love and affection from others because connection is a human need we all can't live without. As soon as that child feels frightened by the people it's trying to get affection from, the child withdraws again. You see this through you having a cycle of unstable relationships where, at times, you are hot and other times cold. This child speaks in many other ways. Maybe the child fears humiliation and failure due to thinking by not doing well. It means rejection is coming. As a result, the child in you makes you avoid taking worthwhile risks by all means possible.

You stay for years in your comfort zone. Trying to be safe and free from ridicule or criticism. But that still doesn't spare the child from hurting. The comfort zone doesn't feel right. The child wants to soar and do well. So, you feel that conundrum from within you as you longingly look at your peers who seem to just be go-getters. They take risks; they progress in life. They push themselves and grow career-wise. Their whole lives seem to be progressive. You take a look at your life and realize that there isn't much progress. Your life is hardly a reflection of your true potential. But why? Who is stopping you from growing? It might seem like it's external resources outside your control, like not having enough resources or other people getting in your way. But if we deeply look at the matter, the truth is that no one and nothing can hold you back unless you let it. This means you have been the one getting in the way of your success. You didn't do this intentionally, of course. All you were trying to do was protect

the child in you from being hurt again. However,

playing it safe has undoubtedly proved to be an unwise survival strategy. It's kept you in your comfort zone. It's boxed you and stopped you from living your life to the fullest.

Upon realizing how much you have been blocking your own progress by playing it safe one way or the other, you may feel very angry at yourself. Before you sink into that dark place, consider this perspective. Do you realize that all you have been doing up until now were things to protect the wounded inner child in you? You didn't want that child to hurt again. To be subjected to the same pain as what happened in the past. So, you did what you knew was best for you up until now. Even though some of the ways you tried to cope were unhealthy and counterproductive, it doesn't change the fact that you have been fighting all your life to protect that vulnerable child whose pain you so vividly recall. It might not have been the best strategy to protect the child that you adopted, but what matters most is that you did something! You have been fighting the good fight.

You might have felt alone numerous times. Perhaps you no longer have a companion you could just trust with that inner child. However, it was hard for you to trust others. Even those who wanted to get close to you. You still looked at them with suspicion as you recalled how people who were meant to protect and love you in your childhood days neglected you when you needed them.

Your understanding of people close to you became that even they might not be reliable at all. So, trust was broken even before you got to give people a chance to show up for you in your present life. Before someone got close to you, you would already believe the story in your head that they are not trustworthy or reliable.

All this can explain why relationships seem to just fail in your life. It's because of the story you learned to believe about yourself and others. You told yourself that story over and over again countless times throughout your life until it became a self-fulfilling prophecy. As you saw people walk away, maybe you didn't stop and critically think why that's happening. As you felt like the same relationship dynamics you experienced when you were a child were repeating themselves in your present life, maybe you didn't open your mind to seeing things from a different perspective. Since chances are that you only trusted yourself, hearing other perspectives that could have been true might have been almost impossible.

Thankfully, reading this book is a sign that you have matured to a point where you realized that to heal and create a new life, maybe it's wise to open your heart to wisdom and learn from others. I would like to commend you for that courage and express my gratitude to you. Thank you for loving yourself enough to never give up. Now, it's time for you to get answers. You might feel like no one ever went through the same experiences you did or would ever understand you. But that's far from reality. The truth is that many people go through similar adverse experiences and childhood traumas. As we explore the topic of attachment styles in this chapter, you will notice that you are not alone at all.

The great news is that once you make sense of your past, healing becomes a lot easier and very much achievable. Another who had childhood wounds and insecure attachment styles can heal and develop a secure attachment style. You can be free from your fears and pain that used to run your life and hold you back. After this chapter, you will be ready to dive fully into your healing and redesign the great life you were always meant to live. It's never too late! The past was just a fraction of your life. Now you have the rest of eternity to step into your authentic self and live a life you will be genuinely happy.

Understanding Different Attachment Styles and How They Develop

Children are born completely dependent on their parents for survival. Any distance from their parents can be distressing, especially in the early days. They form their attachment to their caregiver in the early years of their lives. This entails the kind of emotional bond developed. John Bowlby, a British psychologist, developed the attachment theory in the late 1960s. It was after he carried out an experiment and saw how newborn babies reacted to their mothers after minutes of being separated. Four distinct attachment styles were observed (Mandriota, 2021):

- Anxious Preoccupied
- Dismissive Avoidant
- Disorganized Fearful Avoidant
- Secure

Babies that showed an anxious attachment style had inconsistent attunement from their mothers. Their needs were met, and then the mother would sometimes leave unexpectedly, and this would make the child very dysregulated. They would also struggle to feel secure even after the parent was back because of worrying that the parent would leave again. Anxiously attached children grow up having low self-worth and viewing others as being better than them. They interpret inconsistent parenting as a sign that they are not worthy of love. Hence, they end up looking outside themselves for love and validation because they inwardly don't believe they are worthy of love. This creates a toxic dynamic where Anxiously attached people always seem to chase people for love and end up being disappointed because no one's love can be a good substitute for self-love. They also tend to abandon themselves in their pursuit of winning other people's validation.

Children who showed the avoidant attachment style lacked emotional attunement. Either they cried or showed discomfort and didn't receive a response at all. Maybe the

parent would show up way later after the child was already exhausted and despondent. Instead of welcoming the parent with joy, the avoidant child starts to avoid their parent due to no longer trusting them. Children who grow up avoidant end up developing hyper-independence, and they also struggle to maintain emotional intimacy due to fearing being abandoned and engulfed.

The fear of being engulfed in relationships comes from situations where the child growing up is forced to look after the parent or feel responsible for their happiness to the point where they can't attend to their needs. Consequently, it makes them grow up feeling very uncomfortable when people are too close to them because they subconsciously worry that the same unhealthy dynamics will repeat themselves. They end up pulling people whenever they crave intimacy and also pushing them away once their fears get activated. Dismissive avoidants end up abandoning other partner or others in relationships due to their extreme need to self-preserve and avoid feeling controlled.

Babies who develop the disorganized fearful avoidant attachment style typically have a parent who is usually chaotic, abusive, and also affectionate sometimes. So they grow up very afraid of people in relationships, and as a result, they can push away others too when their fears activate. However, the moment they sense distance, they start trying to get close to you again due to the confusing conundrum they find themselves in, where they know that they can also get affection from the same person who abuses or treats them poorly.

As people grow up, these attachment styles continue to show their pretty or ugly faces in relationships. All insecure attachment styles cause a lot of heartache in relationships. The bond is often not strong and healthy. There is a lot of emotional volatility, which a secure person can find to be very destabilizing and unbearable. If someone with an insecure attachment style pairs up with someone who is securely attached, their negative outlook on life and attachment style can end up causing the securely attached person to either be avoidant, anxious, or also have a disorganized attachment style depending on how they were treated.

This shows that when trauma isn't healed, it

makes you suffer, and other people you come across end up suffering from your wounds, too. The cycle repeats itself over and over again until someone courageous puts in the work and raises children who are securely attached.

Babies that develop a secure attachment style feel safe and well-attuned to their parents. They would cry or show discomfort, and their needs would be met. This would subconsciously teach them that the world is a safe place and that they are worthy of having their needs met including receiving love.

It would also make them feel safe about being independent and exploring their world more because they would know that if anything happens and they cry out, they are likely to get a response. Ultimately, their early experiences make them grow up as self-assured, expressive, emotionally mature, and healthy people. They trust people and tend to enjoy interdependence in their relationships.

Without emotional awareness, it's impossible to notice and understand how children's trauma related to how your caregivers treated you might still be negatively impacting your relationships. You are likely to repeat the same survival strategies in your relationships and suffer from the same wound unless you amass the courage to face your past and work on developing a secure attachment.

Most people who are insecurely attached tend to be very unaware of the toxic habits they use to try to protect themselves from their fears. This makes them attract the same relationship and have history repeat itself in their current lives. To short-circuit that cycle and put an end to the childhood trauma and pain caused by adverse childhood experiences, let's now dive into exploring ways you can heal. Healing means learning to be true to yourself and no longer leaving out of fear. It's having emotional clarity and learning to express and stand up for your needs while also showing up for others in a balanced way. It means learning to develop sincere, quality connections with others and, most importantly, with yourself.

How to Heal and Develop a Secure Attachment Style

It's definitely possible to heal from any unhealthy attachment style. What's important is remembering that your attachment style was your way of adapting to the unsafe feelings you had. You did what you knew best then to protect yourself. However, those coping mechanisms don't have to continue to define you or influence your behaviors. When you were a child, it was understandable that you ended up acting in those ways and couldn't do anything more because you were still a dependent. For example, if you are an avoidant, you might have learned to shut down your emotions just so that you won't be judged, dismissed, or abandoned. If you were anxiously attached, you might have felt the need to be a people-pleaser just so you could get the reassurance and love you desperately needed.

Nevertheless, now that you are an adult, you cannot continue to think in ways that jeopardize your freedom. Unlike a helpless child, you now can meet your needs in healthy ways. You no longer have to employ maladaptive strategies to survive. Recognize and acknowledge that there are better ways to do things. Prepare your mind and heart to face the truth and no longer live in the imagined fear of abandonment.

The first step in healing from insecure

attachment styles is to develop holistic self-awareness. You have to know yourself for who you really are. You can also start to identify your emotions and make an effort to understand them.

Notice your behavioral patterns and start questioning why you act that way. Keep asking yourself why until you get to the underlying root core beliefs you developed about yourself and others, which drive your thoughts and actions. Some of those core beliefs may be true.

However, most core beliefs people develop after experiencing trauma tend to be quite warped and irrational. For instance, you might

develop a belief that people generally don't like you and that you are defective. We all have flaws, but to see yourself as damaged good isn't a healthy thing to be okay with accepting. That belief can drive you into settling for the bare minimum in relationships and not attracting any abundance in your life. It can fuel learned helplessness, leading to you living way below your potential and still being unaffected as much by it because of believing that you can't do any better.

To help you fully identify and understand the key characteristics of each attachment style, here is a summary (Cherry, 2023b):

Signs of Anxiously Preoccupied Attachment Style:

- tend to be codependent
- fear abandonment more than anything
- overly dependent on external validation
- struggle to self-soothe and tend to overly rely on others for their emotional regulation
- extremely afraid of rejection
- usually clingy in relationships
- feel very unworthy of love
- struggle with low self-esteem
- due to their fragile sense of self-worth, they tend to be very sensitive to criticism
- don't easily trust
- always craving for approval or compliments from others
- can at times have jealous tendencies

Signs of Dismissive Avoidant Attachment Style:

- have a background of being left to look after themselves

- might have been reprimanded or humiliated for being dependent or asking for their needs to be met
- may have been mistreated whenever they tried to express their needs
- having caregivers who were very slow to attend to their needs
- grow up believing they don't need others and can make it on their own
- usually alone
- don't feel comfortable with people getting too close to them even though they do desire intimacy
- tend to push away people and dismiss their needs and emotions
- don't trust people easily
- tend to pride themselves on being independent but secretly also feel empty and sad that they live isolated lives
- struggle to compromise; they feel like people force them to sacrifice what matters to them
- afraid of vulnerability due to having painful memories of being mistreated whenever they expressed vulnerability in their early years
- avoid intimacy, especially emotional

- have a hard time understanding their emotions or being emotionally available to others
- sensitive to criticism
- often self-absorbed, people feel alone in relationships with them
- can ghost or abandon people from nowhere whenever their fears get activated

Signs of Disorganized Fearful Avoidant Attachment Style:

- grew up with caregivers who were sources of your comfort and pain
- extreme fear of rejection
- acting every hot and cold, confused love
- having a hard time trusting people
- feeling very afraid of people you love

- often show traits of both anxious and dismissive, avoidant attachment style
- have a hard time regulating your emotions
- can end up acting abusive, like how your caregivers used to abuse or mistreat you
- poor boundaries
- low self-esteem
- inability to form secure attachments, often inconsistent

Signs of Secure Attachment Style:
- have great interpersonal skills
- self-awareness
- interdependent
- comfortable being vulnerable and intimate
- healthy self-esteem
- emotionally available for themselves and others
- possess great self-regulation skills
- good at receiving constructive feedback and self-reflecting
- effectively manage conflicts
- usually in their true frame
- okay with being alone
- comfortable asking for help when necessary

Healing Strategies

Before treating any ailment, the first step is to always correctly diagnose what's wrong. Once you know what your attachment style is and what caused it, it's easier to start implementing healing techniques to help you overcome your past trauma.

Having insecure attachment styles is a sign that your childhood was traumatic, and that's why you ended up attaching to people the way you do. As shared previously, the great news is that you can certainly change your behavioral and thought patterns. Your mindset doesn't have to continue to be an extension of your childhood trauma anymore.

Below are suggested strategies to help you develop a secure attachment style.

Step 1: Acceptance

Accepting that something is wrong is what's needed to unfold the healing process. The more you continue to be defensive or pretend to be happy with the way you handle things, the further you will be from healing and becoming the best version of yourself. Acceptance means having the courage to face all of who you really are.

Trauma makes us take on a "false self." We

hide behind the new maladaptive personalities we created to survive. Remember that what makes it hard to love yourself and have healthy relationships is that who you act like is not even a true representation of the real you. So that's why you feel disconnected  from yourself and find it hard to have fulfilling relationships that feel safe. You probably worry that people will find out who you really are and all your insecurities, and hence why you play hot and cold games or settle for shallow relationships where you don't allow anyone to truly see you. Begin to accept all your wounds and remember that they don't make you any less valuable or worthy of love. When you start accepting yourself for where you are now, you short-circuit the cycle of attracting rejection. When we reject ourselves, whether subconsciously or overtly, we also attract people who reject us. Conversely, when you start accepting and no longer harshly judging yourself, you will also attract more acceptance and compassion from others.

Step 2: Forgiveness

This is a huge step. It's not something you

should force yourself to do overnight. What matters is getting the process started so that you can let go of the bitterness and resentment possibly stored in your heart. You probably feel angry and hurt that your caregivers didn't love and treat you the way you deserved. You may feel like they messed you up and robbed you of a great life you could have had. You might be blaming and accusing them a lot for what they did. This mentality makes it hard for you to operate on a good and high frequency. You become sour, and that hurt can seep into many of your relationships as you unknowingly also perpetuate the unhealthy cycles of hurting others.

Unforgiveness prolongs the loneliness and abandonment you feel. Therefore, it's important to remember that for you to have the love and security of healthy relationships, you always longed for, you have to let go of unforgiveness since it blocks intimacy and causes you to ignore many opportunities for rebuilding healthy relationships.

What's even more important is remembering that unforgiveness frees you from the bondage of living in resentment. Sadness and stress never leave people who hold on to unforgiveness. To set yourself free and find your lasting joy again, practice letting go.

To ensure that forgiveness takes place sincerely and from the heart, you have to give your pain a voice. There are many things you wished to say that you might have lived in fear of expressing. To truly be free from that pain, you have to pour your heart into your loved ones and anyone who hurt you. Even if they don't respond well, that's not what should matter. What's most important is that you get to exercise showing up for that inner wounded child inside you who was so afraid to speak up or who got dismissed. As you share your story, don't expect people to validate your pain; you validate your own pain by sharing it.

You can also start by writing down your story and reading it out loud to yourself. Become the parent who gets to safely take care of the inner child hurting inside you.

Once you have expressed your hurt, get ready for the next step: repairing the relationship you have with yourself and others.

Step 3: Visualize Your New Life

Now that you have unearthed your past pain, stood up for yourself, and made amends with the past, it's time to look forward and no longer live your life facing the rearview mirror.

Wherever your focus goes, energy will always flow in that direction. The point of this step is to stop allowing any of your focus and energy to be pumped in the wrong direction anymore. You may not have had control over your past, but now you have full control of your present and future, and it's up to you to recreate the life of your dreams. The power and responsibility of helping lie in your hands, meaning you have full control of what your life story will now become.

This step is about strategizing how you will now treat yourself well so that you can develop a secure attachment style because of the way you represent yourself. Remember, previously, we learned that babies that develop a secure attachment style end up being that way because of how their parents loved them. Now, you get the chance to be your caregiver. Now, you can give your inner child a chance to receive the unconditional and consistent love, respect, care, attention, and affection they always longed to have. Imagine how exciting that is! You can give yourself the limitless love that will help you to feel self-assured and have healthy relationships with others.

Start creating routines and plans for how you will take care of yourself. What are the daily activities you will do to meet your needs moving forward? What are your needs? What are the values and principles you would like to live by moving forward? What are your boundaries, and how will you communicate them to others and maintain them? What are your dreams and purpose? What do you enjoy doing? What do you dislike? What would you like to explore about yourself? What have you always to be and do? What's stopping you? What can you do to make a way to achieve your goals and dreams? What are you afraid of? How will you face those fears?

This is the part where you have to put in a lot of work to redesign your life and write down a blueprint of the life you want to create for yourself. Take some time to meditate and think deeply about this, and keep updating your vision as more answers keep coming to you. Use the above questions as guidelines to help you envision and redesign your life.

Step 4: Action Out Your Plan

The next step is to implement your plans. All your goals have to be time-bound. You can set short- and long-term goals of what you would like to accomplish. Every area of your life needs to be well-balanced; there shouldn't be negligence in any aspect of your life. The key is to now practice living a life where you are truly attuned and connected with your needs. Every dismissed need or emotion will only hurt you even more.

Make sure that your health, relationships, recreational life, career, family, dreams, spiritual life, and mental health are well catered for. Conduct weekly evaluation sessions where you assess how things are going and adjust what needs to be adjusted accordingly.

This stage is the habit formation stage. It's the time when you have to let go of old habits and press forward to create new ones. It takes time, about three weeks on average, for the brain to get used to new habits and form established neural pathways that will reinforce those new habits. Your goal should be to never give up within those first weeks. It only gets easier with time. Even if you do falter here and there, don't be hard on yourself. Keep trying; as long as you don't give up, you are still going to be on the winning path.

Our brains are built very uniquely with special abilities to adapt and change. As you form new habits, your brain will be engraving them into your new being through the process called neuroplasticity. 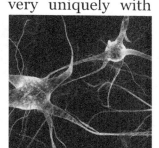 Simply put the brain changes based on how you train it (through adopting new habits).

You can also journal your process and take some time to celebrate your small wins along the way. Don't wait for perfection to come before you can start being proud of yourself. There is no such thing! The whole excitement and fun lies in making the most of your journey and enjoying every step along the way.

Yes, you will have times when you might relapse and return to old habits, but just keep going. You will learn what works better and what doesn't through trial and error. Always exercise self-compassion and be your biggest cheerleader.

Think about how a loving parent would treat their child who is learning new things for the first time; that parent won't reprimand or reject the child for making mistakes. The parent just wants what's best for the child and offers all the necessary support and encouragement. The child also doesn't take to heart their mistakes. They just keep going until they master whatever new skill they are trying to acquire.

Children also learn a lot from observation. You can also adopt the same strategy and try your best to emulate people who model the behaviors and mindsets you wish to have. Become that loving and encouraging parent to your inner child who only cheers them on. This will silence any previous patterns of negative self-talk and create a new, loving way for you to communicate with yourself.

Examples of habits you can practice healing your inner child include:

- Practicing saying "no" if you don't want to do something or agree with it.
- Speaking your truth always, even if you are worried it might offend someone.
- Being intentional about creating deep bonds with others, making the first move.
- Taking time to understand and process your emotions instead of shutting them down.

- Create a well-balanced life, and don't forget to have fun.
- Practice healthy self-regulation strategies like taking nature walks, listening to music, and asking to confide in a trusted friend.
- Speak well of people who hurt you, and let go of the old story.
- Give what you want to receive from others.
- Practice being fully present with yourself and others.
- Become a great listener; start by listening to yourself well.
- Create a routine and be disciplined to stick to it.
- Delay gratification, do things the right way.
- Avoid using unhealthy coping mechanisms to deal with your emotional pain, e.g., isolating yourself, pretending you are okay, people-pleasing.
- Set and enforce your boundaries assertively.
- Focus on learning how to love and validate yourself instead of expecting others to do it for you.
- Explore the world, and try new things.

- Practice communicating your needs effectively.
- Do things that challenge your fears.
- Ask for help when you need it.
- Use affirmations to plant new healthy beliefs and thoughts in your mind.
- Eat well.
- Exercise regularly.
- Get adequate sleep.
- Spoil yourself from time to time.
- Respect your time, and avoid procrastinating.
- Let go of negative self-talk and ruminate on what happened to you in your childhood.

Step 5: Develop and Nurture a Strong Support Network

You can go far by trying to do things alone,

but you will go even way further if you open your heart to allowing others to be there for you too. Start to create and nourish new relationships with friends and family members who care about you. Invest your time and energy into building those connections so that there is mutual respect and reciprocal support. Practice giving and receiving love in those relationships. Being in actual relationships with different people gives us the real-life training and experience we need to overcome our bad habits and become better people.

Be open to receiving feedback from others. Self-reflect and always find ways to better yourself. Share your struggles with others and ensure that you are not hyper-independent or too dependent in the relationships. Practice balanced self-regulation and mutual healthy dependency.

When your fears are activated, instead of leaving into your old coping mechanisms and catering to those fears, be vulnerable and share with your loved ones about your struggle so that they can support you and also not take your behavior personally.

Consider also working closely with a professional such as a counselor, mentor, or therapist to help you heal even faster and gain perspective. They, too, can be a part of your support network.

Step 6: Practice Mindful Living

Our traumas cause us to live most of our lives looking behind us or worrying too much about the uncertain future such that we can forget to be fully present in the "now." This can create a cycle of always feeling like you are behind in your own life and unable to keep pace and manage your daily responsibilities.

Mindfulness is the practice of focusing on the present and living with intention. Instead of allowing your mind to wander in all sorts of places, start taking control. Practice Being in your true frame and being fully present. If you feel distracted, take a break and empty your mind through the process of meditation, writing, or talking about what's bothering you.

Focus on winning each day at a time. Don't live your life always being plagued with worries and anxieties about what happened before or what you don't have control over. Your gift is today; make it count.

If you live this way, you will look back one day and be astounded at the enormous progress you made by just living one day at a time and training your mind to focus on "today." That mentally frees you from being controlled by your past or future.

Step 7: Let Go of All Limitations

Growing up, you probably gave yourself labels of who you are and what you can do. Other people might also have told you what you can and cannot do. They may have given you labels like, "You aren't good at sport" or "You are a shy person." These are the kinds of labels you now have to question and challenge.

This stage is an ongoing stage where you now have to live the rest of your life detoxing from any unhealthy and unnecessary limitations in your life. Unplugging yourself from wrong core beliefs, thoughts, habits, words, and company should be your lifetime practice. Just as we all have to clean our homes every day and throw away any waste, you too have to clean up your mind and life every day by letting go of anything that doesn't serve you.

Step 8: Enjoy Your New Life and Be Grateful

Realize how you are no longer a victim of

your past. Isn't it wonderful to look back at your journey and see how much growth you have experienced and will continue to? Now it's time to fall in love with everything about your life and who you are. Replace complaints and grumbling with gratitude. Always find things to be grateful for and kill the negative bias that might lure you to focus on negative things.

Life will always be full of challenges, but if you have the right mindset, you can always use those challenges as stepping stones to a more meaningful life.

Begin to serve and help others heal from their pain, too. Giving people what you always wanted to have brings deeper levels of healing and satisfaction in your soul, too.

Now that we have unpacked how you can dive deeply into your healing process, it's time to grow even more. The next chapters will help you how to master important strengths, such as knowing how to love yourself and be your most authentic and confident self. Ready to get started? Let's go!

CHAPTER 4
LIVING MINDFULLY AND LEARNING TO LOVE YOURSELF FULLY

The life you used to live before facing the pain of your hurting inner child was probably a life of merely trying to survive instead of thriving. It's hard and almost impossible to love yourself when your inner child's feelings and needs are exiled or suppressed.

You lived a life mainly led by your fears instead of healthy beliefs. Navigating your new life as the mature and more healed version of you will require you to re-assess your core beliefs and form new habits that will help your inner child feel safe and learn to trust you as their new capable and adult protector.

You might have gotten so accustomed to minimizing yourself, allowing people to walk over you, not having clear boundaries, and living a people-pleasing life in an attempt to protect your ego and gain validation. This pattern disconnects you from the true desires and feelings of your heart. You become your own bully in your own life. When people see you treating yourself that way, it also teaches them how to treat you. You will likely have a hard time attracting love and respect if you don't give love and respect to yourself first. You are bound to be dismissed and undermined in your personal and professional life if you have made it a habit to downplay yourself and dismiss your strengths.

Thus, your life becomes a mirror of how you treat yourself. At face value, it might have looked like it was other people's fault why you weren't happy or making it as far as you could. However, in hindsight, you can notice the link between what you accept for yourself and what ends up being the reality of your life. If you settle for the bare minimum in your relationships, that's all that most people in your life are likely to sow into you. However, if you make it clear that you deserve more and sow the seeds to reap more in every domain of your life, there is no way that a harvest of abundance won't come your way.

This chapter will teach you lessons to help you take radical responsibility for your life. It will inspire you to create the change you desire to see in every aspect of your life. It all starts with learning to heal the relationship you have with yourself. Once you build a healthy relationship with yourself, that relationship will become a blueprint or standard of how all your other relationships are meant to be. The idea that we attract what we are is no myth. We can only invite the love, stability, peace, respect, happiness, and harmony we long for into our lives when we first learn to gift ourselves those attributes before anyone else can.

Having said that, are you now ready to get started with making over your life such that it will be a true reflection of your worth and myriad talents and gifts? Let's get started.

Developing Emotional Awareness

Our emotions are beautiful, and important messages are gifted to us to help us stay connected to our needs. They remind us how we feel when our needs are being violated or respected or when our values are being dismissed.

Childhood neglect causes many of us to disconnect from our true emotions. This makes it hard for you to know what you need and even who you are. You end up lying to yourself or forcing yourself to fit in just to feel needed or loved. However, living this way does not create a healthy foundation for developing a great relationship with yourself and others. How can people love and respect you if you are disconnected from your true self? How can others trust you if you change and easily morph yourself into anything or anyone just to avoid rejection? Disconnecting with our emotions makes us lose credibility and a sense of groundedness. We become like dry leaves being tossed about by the wind in any direction and at any time.

The first step in developing emotional awareness is to practice being true to yourself. Let's review the steps below to learn how to connect with your true feelings and develop better self-awareness.

Acknowledging Your Inner Child Feelings

Think about what it takes to know how someone feels. You make time to listen to them attentively. This gives you the chance to read their verbal and non-verbal communication to fully understand what they are going through. Similarly, for you to connect with your true feelings, you have to give your inner child quality time and just listen to them. Your emotions are stored in your inner child's consciousness.

You can give your inner child a platform to speak by writing a letter to your adult self on their behalf. In that letter, allow your inner child to tell you their raw emotions, what they want, what makes them happy, what upsets them, their dreams, and so on. Let that inner child express their frustrations to your adult self because, chances are, your inner child probably had a hard time trusting you and feels neglected up until now. To build a trusting relationship between you and your inner child, they first have to know that you will hear them out and no longer dismiss their needs. Listen without interrupting or imposing your adult opinions on the inner child. Just let them be and listen to their untold story.

Keep in mind that your inner child may have different emotional states. Sometimes, they might sound upset, other times playful, and other times, maybe even sassy. Just listen to them with an open and compassionate heart. Immerse yourself in your inner child's feelings and remember those raw feelings you often hide from people. That letter from your inner child to your adult self now can sound something like this:

Dear Adult Self,

It must have taken you a lot of courage to

finally open and listen to me,

What took you so long? I felt so suffocated and unloved every time you ignored me.

I tried to tell you that dismissing me would never make you happy, but you're so stubborn and full of fear that you chose to live an inauthentic life.

Why do you doubt yourself so much? Remember all my strengths. You hardly ever used any of them to create the life we deserve.

Did you know that I was the coolest kid and also the smartest at school? You probably forgot because you chose to listen to naysayers and haters instead of following your heart and truth. Now look, we have been reduced to living an average, boring, isolated, and painful life.

You spend most of your time chasing love and pleasing people who don't even care about you. Why do you do that? I care about you, but you ignore me and make me feel like I'm not good enough for you. You would rather be loved by others than focus on learning to love yourself.

How does that make any sense, though? You expect people to love you when you don't love yourself. I am you! The way you treat me is exactly how you treat yourself.

Can you please also stop using all sorts of external achievements to mask your miserable life? There's no amount of money or fake relationships that can give us the happiness we need when we are just free to be ourselves.

Who you are is beautiful. Please believe in me. I need you to stop mistreating me. If you don't stop, I will scream out loud in many ways until I get your attention. That can look like you end up being sick or mentally ill. I don't want that for you because I am you. It will just hurt me to see you keep on suffering. But something has to be done to get you to listen to me.

Can we just be friends and embrace this gift of life together? I would like to join you as your partner, not an angry self, protesting against

your choices.

I hope to hear from you soon. Please take action before it's too late. I love you. Hope you believe me.

With love,

Your inner child.

Wouldn't reading that letter make you tear up? This is an example of allowing your inner child to express their feelings. All you have to do after reading their letter is to acknowledge their feelings. Apologize where you have to. Respond with empathy. Assure your inner child that you will protect and not neglect them again. Words matter, but what will truly make your inner child feel validated is when you consistently prove through your thoughtful actions that you are now there for them.

Meditate and Journaling

Carve out time each day to talk to your inner child. Make it part of your daily routine. Do emotional check-in sessions with them. This is when you get to tap into your raw feelings and listen intently to what your inner child is telling you. Remember, your inner child is a true representation of who you are. That person wants to be seen, heard, and loved. Furthermore, your inner child wants to explore life adventures and work alongside you. Integrating your inner child into who you are now will help you feel truly connected to yourself. Once you reach this point, you begin to love yourself because you are being truly connected to the real you.

Meditation means being still and concentrating your thoughts on specific subjects or a certain thought or memory. You can plan your meditation sessions, for example:

- **Monday's topic**: Remembering games I enjoyed playing when I was young.
- **Tuesday's topic:** Unearthing and examining my core beliefs.
- **Wednesday's topic:** Creating new healthy core beliefs and writing affirmations to help me reinforce them.
- **Thursday's topic:** Unplugging from all the negative words I was told that are still attached to my soul.
- **Friday's topic:** Reviewing my self-talk and using positive affirmations to replace unkind words I say to myself.
- **Saturday's topic:** Coming up with a comprehensive list of new adventures I must explore.
- **Sunday's topic:** Tapping into my anger and bitterness. Letting go of past hurt and forgiving those who wounded me.

Sounds great, right? You can switch up the topics as you see fit. The more you listen to your inner child, the more you will know what that child needs you to address. You can add the topic they tell you about to your meditation schedule. It doesn't have to take long. Ideally, 30 minutes of spending quality time with yourself, meditating, and journaling would be best. However, you can still do it

for a shorter time frame. Play calm, soothing music as you meditate to help you sink deep into your memories and thoughts and tap into your creativity.

Inject Playfulness Into Your Life

Your inner child wants to have fun. Most adults can end up making themselves live miserable lives because they block the playful side of themselves. Who wrote a rule that being an adult means you can't have fun? If you are following that invisible rule, maybe consider changing your ways.

Part of the suppressed emotions of your inner child is the need to be carefree and play. Remember how children tend to just get along with anyone. They can make friends easily and also get over other people's mistakes easily. Return to that enjoyable and adventure-filled way of being. Practice making friends with others and letting go of offenses instead of harboring bitterness. That will restore to your soul that essence of purity and being adorable, which we love about children.

Don't hide behind chores and work and use that as an excuse for not making time to play. Practice effective time management skills to create a work-life balance and carve out time for fun activities.

Learn About Emotional Intelligence

One of the best ways to build a healthy relationship with yourself and others is to develop your emotional intelligence (EQ). This refers to your ability to deeply understand and appropriately respond to your emotions and those of others.

Five key components of emotional intelligence include being self-aware, having the ability to self-regulate effectively, having interpersonal skills, having empathy, and being self-motivated.

- **Self-awareness:** This refers to your knowledge of your true emotions, feelings, thoughts, values, standards, flaws, weaknesses, strengths, and so on. Self-awareness comes in two forms: public and private self-awareness. To develop healthy relationships with others, you have to know how people perceive you; that's public self-awareness. On the other hand, private self-awareness is being in touch with how you feel inside. Other people may be clueless about your internal state. An example of private self-awareness is knowing that you are scared of losing your partner in a relationship. Your partner might not know that you have that fear, but only you might know it. Listening to trustworthy feedback and pondering on your habits and emotions can help you develop a good idea of who you holistically are. Doing inner child healing work like you are now also helping to grow your self-awareness.

- **Self-regulation:** We all have to take responsibility for our emotions. Self-regulation is coming up with practices or things to do to help you effectively manage your emotions. This means instead of just yelling at people or acting moody all day when you are upset; you resort to healthy practices to self-soothe. Examples are doing breathing exercises, meditating, exercising, journaling, listening to calming music, making your favorite meal, or talking to a trusted friend who can help you feel better. Self-regulation doesn't mean that you always have to do it alone. You can be interdependent and allow others to support you if they can.

- **Interpersonal Skills:** These social skills help you build meaningful relationships with others. Examples include learning how to communicate effectively, joining different hobbies and doing volunteer projects, offering to help people in their daily challenges, loving others in their preferred love language, and having good boundaries.

- **Empathy:** This refers to your ability to step outside your perspective momentarily and put yourself in other people's shoes. It's hard to be in a relationship with someone who is always self-absorbed and unwilling or unable to show any consideration for your perspective. You can end up feeling alone and underappreciated. Children who face negligence often struggle to empathize since they don't see that behavior being modeled to them. If that's your case, please don't be hard on yourself. It just means that now you have to accept that you lack that skill and be open to learning how to develop it. Don't insist on being right when people tell you they don't feel loved or heard when they are with you. A great place to start is to watch fictional movies or real-life stories that have characters who are good at practicing empathy. Even reading or listening to podcasts can help you develop your critical thinking skills, which in turn opens your mind to understanding perspectives other than your own. Working closely with a therapist can also help you harness cognitive behavioral therapy (CBT) to break free from negative behavioral patterns and adopt new healthy relational habits.

- **Motivation:** What usually gets you pumped up to get things done and achieve better goals? Do you always have to wait for something outside yourself to inspire you to take action, or are you able to stir yourself into action? People with high EQ tend to be very good at motivating themselves. You, too, can develop that skill by believing more in yourself and harnessing the tools you have around you. For instance, listening to music, reading encouraging quotes, watching an inspirational movie, or exercising can get you motivated to take action on your goals and dream bigger. Lean in more into those activities and more instead of only waiting for someone else to make you feel good and get you ready to be productive. Childhood trauma can cause you to learn helplessness, whereby you believe that you can't do anything to change your life. You start to expect someone else to be your hero. What if that person never comes? Will you just keep waiting? Even if they do, expecting other people to be responsible for your success is unfair. Take ownership of your life and realize that you are born with greatness within you. It's just waiting for you to put in the work of unlocking it and letting it shine.

Practice Setting and Keeping Healthy Boundaries

Not sure if your boundaries are good or not? Asking these leading questions can help you understand your strengths and weaknesses when it comes to boundary setting.

Do you have a hard time standing up for yourself, especially when people catch you off-guard? Do social interactions overwhelm you,  *maybe due to feeling like people end up invading your personal space and privacy? Do you feel like people tend to try to control you or even tell you how you are supposed to feel? Does your family or loved ones have many unhealthy expectations for you and punish you in some way if you don't fulfill their needs? Are you often abandoning yourself just to please others and be liked? Do you speak up for yourself when people are making false or rude claims about you? Do you always feel the need to say yes because you think saying no might reinforce your fear of being seen as a bad person? Do you over function in your relationships and attract people who tend to be takers rather than mutually reciprocate love and respect? Are you always overworking to try to prove your worth? Do you suppress your true emotions just to "keep the peace and not upset others?" Does your life reflect your true potential, or do you just settle for less? Do people respect your time and presence?*

As a child, your core wound might have been being told that there is something wrong with you. Believing this makes you feel defective and not worthy of love or respect. It creates a core belief in your psyche that you aren't worth much. This belief is what then makes you enable others to treat you badly. It makes you settle for less even though deep down in your soul, your inner child might remind you from time to time that you are believing lies.

You can even believe another malignant idea that no one will ever love you. This can make you settle for toxic or abusive relationships, because in your head, being with someone even though they mistreat you is better than not having anyone loving you at all. That's why it's important to uproot all negative limiting beliefs you might have, that cause you to have weak boundaries. Whatever we believe about ourselves is what people will sense and reflect on us. Just like how most dogs tend to be aggressive when they notice that you are afraid of them... Believing the worst about yourself also makes people mistreat you. That's why the first step in building healthy b boundaries is letting go of toxic beliefs and adopting healthy core beliefs. Let's explore more on that.

Uproot Unhealthy Limiting Beliefs and Build Empowering and Positive Beliefs

Do you remember what you were told about how you were treated, which made you feel like you were less than good enough? Who said those mean words to you? Do you think that person loved? Chances are, they were only projecting their self-hate or bitterness on you. So, you took things personally and were conditioned to believe that what they said about you was true. You might have even convinced yourself that you deserved to be neglected, abused, or given breadcrumbs in your childhood.

Letting go of that negative conditioning can free you from other people's baggage you might have taken as your own. Write down what those negative beliefs were. Also, try to trace the root cause of your behavioral patterns. For instance, why do you avoid social interactions or fear intimacy? Asking these questions can help you find certain answers like perhaps you were made to believe that you aren't lovable, or you will just embarrass yourself. So, you end up settling for a life that feels like you're imprisoned and trapped in many limitations.

Replace every core belief you have with positive and empowering beliefs that can help you counter the counterproductive activities or habits you have. Use affirmations to plant those new beliefs in you. Also, practice being the person you wish to be; doing this consistently will eventually rewire your brain programming and make you an entirely different and healthier version of yourself.

Set New Values for Yourself

If you don't have standards for how you want to be treated by others, people will just do whatever they want with you. That's why it's important to have clear values and communicate them in advance to others. There should also be consequences for those who happen to violate those values and boundaries knowingly. If you don't exercise the consequences you announced, people won't take your boundaries seriously anymore. It trains them to keep repeating the very behaviors that hurt you. They do that because they know they can get away with it.

An example of value and boundary you can set is saying something like, "I don't respond to that volume and attitude," when someone is yelling at you. Further, communicate what the consequences of them yelling to you will be, such as "If you keep raising your voice at me and being rude, I will walk away. Only speak to me when you are ready to have a respectful conversation." The time will certainly come for you to be tested. People will watch to see if you will honor your words. The moment you stay there and allow people to yell at you without walking away as you promised, that's going to be your recurring reality for a long time unless you put your foot down. It takes practice to get comfortable with applying healthy boundaries. At first, your voice might be shaky as you assert yourself, but more practice makes things perfect. Your inner child will also be watching you stand up for yourself, and this will build self-trust and bring healing to your soul. Keep repeating your boundaries until it's clear to others what you stand for.

Don't Dim Your Light to Make Others Comfortable

Another way to set healthy boundaries is to respect your greatness and potential. When you play small, you are dimming your light just to try to get validation from others. Think about it: If someone truly cared about you, would they be happy with seeing you undermine your worth and potential? No. They will encourage you to do your best and shine your light. This means that you have to have healthy boundaries with yourself. Know your worth and accept it. Know what you are capable of and go for it! Don't put off what you can do today until tomorrow that will only delay your success. The more you own your greatness and let go of the need to impress people who might not even care about you, the more you will set yourself free from living in mediocrity. Better to be alone or have few friends than to be surrounded by people who put you down and feel comfortable when you downplay yourself.

This brings us to the conclusion of this chapter. Learning how to have a healthy relationship with yourself is an ongoing work with no end. Each day is a new opportunity to show up for your inner child like you have never done before. You can break free from self-hate or toxic relationships by learning to love, appreciate, and respect yourself. Let's now move forward to the next chapter, where we will explore how you can populate your new life with pleasant memories and worthwhile pursuits.

CHAPTER 5
BUILDING HEALTHY RELATIONSHIP

Trauma makes us have tumultuous relationships. It's hard to have stable connections when you don't know how to be authentic with yourself and others. This brings tremendous anguish to our souls. Human beings have an inherent need for connection. When we are deprived of true connection, we become anxious and unfulfilled.

Sometimes, we may try to replace that pain with chasing after material needs, trying to be hyper-independent, or using career success as a cover for our pain. However, none of those things can fill the void in our hearts, which can only be filled with authentic and healthy bonds.

After having a childhood that made it hard for you to trust others and also doubt your worth, how do you heal and transition into building healthy relationships? The previous chapters helped us recognize how important it is to nurture your self-love. That becomes the foundation of building healthy relationships. It's utterly impossible to attract healthy interactions when we don't interact with ourselves in healthy ways. Implementing the knowledge in the previous chapters and starting to love yourself first will make it possible to change your frequency and vibration such that you will be able to enjoy secure and lasting relationships.

Think about how the television works. If you want to listen to the music channel you can't stay on the cartoon network. You have to change the channel for you to hear music. Waiting for hours and days watching cartoon networks won't allow you to get what you want just because you are waiting patiently for it. You have to take action and go to the channel that allows you to access music. Similarly, not loving ourselves and expecting healthy and authentic bonds is futile. No matter how hard you chase people, sacrifice yourself, and try to please others, you won't have true and healthy connections unless you bridge the gap of self-love deficiency.

This is in line with the universal laws of

nature. For instance, if you jump up, you will certainly fall because of the law of gravity. It doesn't matter who you are or what you believe about that law. It will still apply to everyone because it's the law of nature. The same goes for the law of attraction. We can only attract what we are. Our lives and relationships become a reflection of how much we have worked on ourselves. It's also like the principle of sowing what we reap. You can't expect to reap cabbages where you planted kale seeds. These examples help us understand why having a healthy relationship is impossible when we haven't learned to have a healthy relationship with ourselves first.

Nurturing Self-Love

We now know that self-love is key to healthy relationships. But you might be asking yourself what self-love practically looks like. *How do I love myself?* That's the big question. For starters, you might want to know that the answer isn't very far from you. Learning and applying all the things we have discussed so far is part of nurturing your self-love! If you didn't love yourself, you would have just remained in your comfort zone and stopped fighting for freedom and the life you deserve. The fact that you are here doing inner child healing work proves that you do love yourself and care about your well-being.

Nevertheless, you can still do plenty of other things to develop a loving, fun, and healthy relationship with yourself. There is also no limit to the number of things you can do to invest in your life and build yourself up such that when you contemplate about your life, you will be proud of the reality you see.

So far, what do you see? Chances are that you mostly see the pain and all the damage that your childhood wounds caused you to have. You feel robbed of the life you could have had. However, self-love demands you to face your past with compassion and use it as a catalyst for achieving the life of your dreams. Instead of being bitter about what you went through, you can choose to look at things differently and use your experiences as a springboard for reaching greater heights. Think about it: There are so many people you can help and connect with because you probably went through what they did, too. It's hard to have a lot of influence on people when all we do is just live a soft life.

People won't be able to relate to you. Thus, your hardships and adverse childhood can widen the circumference of people that you can connect with.

Your past only represents a fraction of your lifetime. That time is over. What remains is an infinite number of years ahead that await you. You can get to choose how you will harness the rest of your life. What you create today and, in your future, can become your new story. Let's now dive into exploring how you can create a great story by employing different habits and practices that help you nurture your self-love.

Refrain From Comparing Yourself to Others

Everyone is running their race. It's utterly unfair for anyone to compare themselves with any other person because we all come from different backgrounds. Start to love yourself by accepting that being different from others is okay. It's okay to not have the same growth pace as others.

The danger of comparing ourselves to others is that we hold ourselves to unrealistic standards of perfection. Especially with the prevalence of social media, people must just show the glamorous side of their lives. You don't get to see how much struggle and pain they are dealing with behind closed doors. You may think that only you have it hard, but life is challenging for everyone. Thus, accept your cross and carry it with grace. Not comparing yourself to others will also help you to accept others for who they are and have compassion for them.

Start to focus more on injecting your time and energy into running your race. As long as you stay in your lane and practice contentment, nothing will easily phase you.

Begin to Value Your Opinion of Yourself More

What caused us incalculable wounds are the unkind opinions from others which, we soak in. We may have believed our caregivers, friends, or family members when they belittled us or called us certain mean names. However, now it's time to declutter all that baggage. You get to chart your course and form your beliefs and values of what you stand for now. No longer allow anyone's opinion of you to define you.

Decide whatever you want to achieve and become in this life and go for it. Let the voices of other people in your head quiet down. Embody everything you envision yourself as and own that truth. Remember that no matter how much success you achieve in this life, people will always have something negative to say anyway. Taking people's opinions to heart will only hinder your growth.

Accept That You Can't Make Everyone Happy

Just as you had to learn to take responsibility for yourself, you also have to allow other people to be responsible for their happiness. Only children deserve our undivided care and protection since they are dependent on us. However, all adults have to take responsibility for themselves. Yes, it's okay to depend on each other in healthy ways. What's wrong is when people disable themselves and expect you to do what they are supposed to do for themselves. If you take it upon yourself to always be responsible for providing everything that people ask you for, it can take a toll on your health. It doesn't also create room for developing healthy relationships with reciprocal support.

Accept that you won't be able to make everyone happy, and that's okay. Do your part to convey your love to others, but know and respect your limits. Sometimes, when people notice that you are willing to abandon yourself to please them, they can take advantage of that and keep exploiting you. Be okay with saying no and show up for yourself more. The more you make sure that your cup is filled first before trying to pour it into others, the easier it will be for you to have a lot more to give without straining yourself.

Permit Yourself to Make Mistakes

Think about how often babies make mistakes while they are growing up and exploring the world. It's what makes them able to learn so much in a short time. However, you may have been reprimanded harshly when you were young for making any mistakes. Maybe it caused you to experience rejection or abuse. That may have made you develop a core belief that you have to be perfect for you to be lovable and accepted. That thought has to be uprooted for you to heal. Whether you make mistakes or not, you are lovable and loved! You are worthy of love and acceptance because you are you.

Start allowing yourself to make mistakes more often. This won't happen if you hold on to being a perfectionist. Most perfectionists hardly take any risks because of failure. Even if they do take risks, they have a hard time accepting their efforts and being proud of themselves. They still feel inadequate. Break free from that vicious cycle by learning to be content with just doing your best one day at a time. Whether things go well or not, that's not what should matter most to you. What ought to be your pride in knowing that you left your comfort zone and dared to try something new? That alone is worthy of praise and honor. Remember that for babies to walk, they had to be willing to fall many times and make mistakes until they figured out how to do it. Similarly, embrace that way of life and also see mistakes as part of your growth process.

Your Body Image Does Not Define Your Worth

Our bodies are just houses where our souls and spirits live. The real you is your spirit, and you have a soul. However, society can put lots of pressure on you to believe that your worth is all about how your body looks. Don't fall into that trap. Love your body, yes, but realize that you are more than what you too like. What makes you special is your spirit and what you bring to this world. Make that your focus and watch how your worth remains solid and unwavering.

Don't Accept Toxicity From People

Remember that people can only treat you the way you allow them to. If someone crosses the line with you, stand your ground and make it clear to them that you aren't a dumping ground for their unacceptable behavior.

People will test you. Make sure you don't fall for any animosity. If someone refuses to respect and honor your values, it's okay to let them go. If it's family members or co-workers, you can keep your distance and refuse to engage in unhealthy behaviors. Asserting your boundaries doesn't make you a bad person. Maybe as a child, you might have been told that you are being selfish by standing up for yourself. Don't fall for those lies anymore. You owe it to yourself to take care of your mental health and sanity.

Face Your Fears

A crucial part of loving yourself is to face your fears and not allow them to control you anymore. Common fears that arise from childhood trauma include fear of abandonment, rejection, failure, and so on. Ask yourself what's the worst thing that can happen if you try to face your fears. When it comes to abandonment issues, remember that as a child, it's valid to have such fears because your survival depends on your caregivers looking after you. However, as adults, it's not okay to continue thinking that you *need* someone to survive. That belief creates an unhealthy dependency on people. As a grown adult, you can look after yourself. Other people's presence in your something should be a pleasure to you. You *want* them, not need them for survival. Being able to accept the difference between needing and wanting someone can help you lessen the extent to which you fear losing them. If they choose to abandon you, reassure your inner child that you will always be there to protect and care for that child.

Any fears we don't face and overcome become the very obstacles that limit us from growing. Usually, fear is all in the thoughts you come up with in your mind about something. It's usually just an illusion. When you do face what you are afraid of, chances are that you will realize that it's not as bad as you imagined it to be.

Rebuild Your Self-Trust

Living a life of dismissing your needs and feelings causes your inner child to not trust you. To rebuild your self-trust, start being fully present with yourself. Practice emotional attunement and listen to how you feel. Think about an appropriate way to respond to your emotions. Whenever you respect yourself, your inner child learns to trust you more.

Self-trust is also built through keeping your promises to yourself. Start setting goals and going after what you truly want. The more you stay disciplined and keep your word, the more your brain learns to also trust you. You begin to also feel great about yourself. Your confidence to achieve higher goals also grows when you continue to show up for yourself.

Seize and Create Opportunities for Success

One mistake many people usually make is waiting for "the right time" to do something. This is a trap to make you waste valuable time. There are always growth opportunities that will arise in every domain of your life. Seize as many as you can. Even though you might have a plan for what you need to do each day, you should still maintain cognitive agility and be open to seizing any opportunities you might not have expected to see.

Having a fixed mindset and only sticking to how you planned everything to work out can make you miss out on important things that come when you don't expect them.

If you notice that opportunities you want aren't showing their face, harnessing your creativity and creating opportunities is okay. There isn't only one way to make it in life. Be open to exploring various ways to get where you want to be, like using a car, bus, bicycle, or motorbike to reach a specific destination. You can also get where you need to be using channels you don't think you would. It might take longer and sometimes faster, but what matters most is that you do make progress.

You Should Always Come First

It's not selfish to ensure that you are fine

before you try to look after everyone else. Think about it: if a mother struggles with mental health issues and neglects herself because she is always busy looking after her child, what happens? Although the child will appreciate her help and devotion, the child will still suffer from the wounds the mother has. Hence, loving herself is also a way of loving and protecting her loved ones. You, too, need to be okay first. Whatever is going on inside you will come out one way or the other. If your heart and spirit are full of joy, you will have a lot of joy to give to others. However, if your spirit is broken and full of bitterness, you will also pour that hurt to others. That's why there is a common saying that "Hurt people are prone to hurt other people too."

Practice Bravery and Boldness

It's easy to practice bravery in secret. However, being bold in public can be challenging. Start to face that fear. For example, when someone is disrespectful to you in public, practice being assertive and standing up for yourself in public, too. This will also teach other people a lesson that you are someone who respects themselves and won't allow people to just get away with unkind behavior towards you.

Social bravery is also something worth

practicing a lot. Instead of isolating yourself or only talking to people you are comfortable with, start conversing with new people. Expand your social circle and go out more. Even if you may feel excluded in some conversations, find a way to politely join in. Walk with confidence, and always remember that anyone who gets to know you is greatly lucky. Don't treat yourself like a fan. Instead, own your uniqueness and treat yourself like someone you admire and love.

Appreciate the Beauty Around You

Sometimes, we live years of our lives tied to the belief that if only we have a nice house, nice car, great romantic relationship, and money, then we will be happy. Attachment to such beliefs can make you fail to see the beauty that's already around you. It blinds you from seeing the beauty in simple things. For instance, being able to wake up healthy, having great weather conditions outside, having food in your pantry, and so on. Start to recognize and be grateful for what you already have. This makes you make the most of all that's already in your hands. Which in turn brings forth more abundance unto your life.

When we take what we have for granted, it doesn't grow, and we don't grow. We also risk losing what we have if we are careless and ungrateful. Thus, let go of your attachment to what life was meant to be like. Accept what you can't change and humbly work on what you can.

Make Kindness One of Your Core Values

Being subjected to abuse or any continual mistreatment makes us more tolerant of bad conduct. It makes us accept being treated unkindly. That pattern now has to stop. Loving yourself means you no longer have to condone any kind of mistreatment either from yourself or others. The world is already full of so much negativity that you don't have to add to it by being critical and harsh to yourself. Cut any negative self-talk and make use of positive  affirmations to help you plant new core beliefs and thoughts that bring you peace and harmony.

Celebrate Yourself Often

Celebrating yourself shouldn't only be limited to your birthdays! Find something to celebrate about yourself each day. You can do this in creative ways like making a delicious meal, pampering yourself, watching your favorite shows, buying yourself cool clothes, upgrading your look, and so on. The more you treat yourself like royalty, the more you will also attract royal treatment from others. Remember, whatever we sow, we always end up reaping that too!

Creative Ideas for Building and Maintaining Great Relationships

All relationships require effort. Just like how you are supposed to plow the ground, weed it, and look after it for plants to grow well, relationships, too, require a consistent effort to grow. People you might have thought you could never be close to may surprise you when you start believing in them and putting in consistent effort to grow better relationships with them.

Is there anyone in your family or friendship circle you wish you had a better relationship with? It's not too late to make that dream come true. Below are some ideas to get you started.

Mutual Support

Healthy relationships require both parties to be there for each other. If only you are giving more while the other is just taking, it will be hard to be happy. To foster mutual support, be authentic, and don't pretend to be okay with everything. Express your needs and try to match each other's energies. Give more to people who invest more in you.

Mature Conflict Management

There are healthy and unhealthy ways to manage conflicts. Unhealthy ways to handle conflict involve things like yelling, gaslighting each other, stonewalling, gossiping, name-calling, threatening to end the relationship, being controlling, and so on. Doing these things doesn't make things better. Rather, focus on healthy conflict management habits such as creating a safe space for open and peaceful dispute settlement, listening to each other, making ground rules for the relationship, having regular emotional check-in sessions to talk about ways to repair things and grow more, being respectful, being assertive, and privately addressing your concerns instead of embarrassing each other in public.

Respect

Respect means learning what the people you are in relationships with value and don't accept. It's honoring their values and boundaries. It's also not trying to control or force them to do what they aren't comfortable with.

Respect also goes along with appreciating someone's contribution to your life. When you always take people for granted, they cease to feel loved and respected. Thus, ensure that you express your gratitude for what others do for you. Politely ask for what you need instead of demanding. Respect also means viewing others as your equal—not assuming that you are better than others. It also involves communicating with decorum and not being passive-aggressive or rude. Things like lying, not keeping your word, and one-sided effort are all signs of disrespect.

Respect should be both ways. You can't just be the only one respecting someone while they trample all over you. If you notice that someone isn't reciprocating your respect, be courageous enough to speak up about it.

Have Balance

Relationships are indeed important, but they

can't be all you invest your time in. You have to manage your life in a way that allows you to have holistic success. Make time to nourish your relationships, but also have ample time to attend to your personal needs and other aspects of your life. You don't have to lose yourself in relationships. Maintain your individuality and also respect the other person's self and interests.

Make Honesty Your Policy

It's better to be disliked for who you are than to be loved for wearing a mask. Allow people to know the real you. This helps you get rid of patterns of isolation and disconnection in your life. Allow people to also show you their authentic selves. Expect to see flaws. There isn't anyone without flaws. Only expecting to be in relationships with perfect people will leave you waiting for a very long time. The key to successful relationships is both parties being willing to work on themselves and put effort into keeping the relationship strong. Be honest and take accountability for any poor decisions or choices you make.

Express Affection

Relationships deprived of affection feel dry and almost robotic. Be in touch with your emotions. When you love someone, show them. Don't just keep that love to yourself. Use varied ways to express your affection. You can either give a physical touch when it's appropriate, give words of affirmation, help them solve their problems, give gifts, or always carve out quality time to nurture the relationship. Something as simple as greeting your friend with a warm, big smile the moment you see them will make them feel loved and wanted.

Support Each Other's Vulnerabilities

When people are vulnerable with you, don't use what they told you against them once you argue. That can kill trust. Be emotionally available for people and even ask them how they would want to be supported by you. Sometimes, you won't have to ask. The more you spend time with someone, the better you know what they need. It's also more special when you surprise people with what they need when they least expect it.

Be Fun and Spontaneous

Relationships get boring when everything is all serious and gloomy. If you constantly have fights, it can strain the relationships and even breed resentment. Be open to exploring activities to do together. Routines are good, but balance them out with spontaneity, and go out to explore various adventures together. The more pleasant memories you have, the stronger your bond will be.

Accept Each Other's Differences

You won't always see eye to eye with people, and that's okay. Learn to see each other's differences as valuable assets to learn from. Don't use them as weapons against each other. Imagine how boring nature would be if there was only one type of plant or flower.  It's the diversity that makes things even more breathtaking. Thus, see how you can use your friends and family members' differences to edify each other.

Another good example is how the body works. Many of your body parts are different, but they work and co-exist well. If everything had the same function, you couldn't do different things.

Work on Effective Communication

Without effective communication, it's impossible to hold up a healthy relationship. Both parties have to learn to communicate in a way that fosters understanding. Don't communicate to hurt the other person. Rather, take a break and get some space to cool down. It helps you avoid doing or saying things you might not be able to reverse. Great communication is all about being a good listener and also effectively making known anything you want to share. This means learning to choose the right time to address certain topics. Speaking in a respectful tone and voice projection. Your body language also has to convey respect.

Practice Self-Regulation

As shared earlier, it's unfair to expect people to always be responsible for how you feel. You, too, shouldn't take responsibility for someone's feelings. If you aren't feeling okay, practice self-regulation exercises to help you clear your mind and cool down. Examples include talking through your feelings with someone, having nature walks, sleeping, swimming, or journaling. Be careful of burdening others with your unprocessed hurt to the point where you end up making people suffer for your wounds. Take active responsibility for your growth and consider doing therapy or listening to self-help content regularly to help you grow and overcome your weaknesses.

Travel Together

Traveling to different cities, countries, or local places together helps you to build memories. Work on saving funds well in advance of your travel date and plan together activities you would like to do. Challenge yourself to include activities you are afraid of.

Give Each Other Constructive Feedback

Relationships give us a great chance to learn a lot about ourselves and grow. When you are isolated, you are unlikely to know in full what your triggers are. You may assume that you have healed from your past. But that only happens because you are secluded. Once you interact with people, that's when you are likely to be triggered sometimes. Don't see this as a bad thing. Your triggers help you to know that something still needs your attention. You can then take action and examine areas in your life where you still need healing. The more triggers that get revealed sooner, the better and faster you will grow!

Empathy

This is one of the most important skills to help you connect deeply with others. Empathy just means understanding where someone else is coming from and feeling what they feel. This makes it possible to be compassionate and more accepting of them. When we only see things from our perspective, we can be judgmental and lack compassion for others. Practicing being a deep listener is a great way to grow your empathy. Take time to understand people's side of the story with an open and curious mind. Ask questions and offer to give your practical support when you can.

Shared Goals

Relationships that last long are those where you have shared goals and learn to work together to accomplish them. The struggles of getting things done bond you even more. Knowing that you are building something with someone makes you find more value in those relationships. Give yourself a timeline for when you would like to have accomplished specific goals. This will also increase your level of interaction since you will have to collaborate to get things done. Continue to challenge yourselves with bigger goals every time you achieve smaller ones.

Small Thoughtful Gestures

Showing people that you are thinking of them and giving pleasant surprises adds sweetness and warmth to relationships. It doesn't have to cost a lot. Even doing something small like writing on the bathroom mirror that you love someone before they wake up to go brush their teeth can be heartwarming. Do more of these small gestures whenever you can. The kindness will always return to you when you also least expect it.

Grow Together

For relationships to last, both parties have to grow. If only a person grows, soon, they may start to feel like they have outgrown the relationship. This can make it hard for you to still get along well together. So, encourage and hold people's hands so they can also grow with you. If they, too, have their own growth goals, take an interest and learn from them. Growing together also keeps the novelty alive in relationships. You continue to be fascinated with each other. Lastly, growing together also means always encouraging each other to never lose sight of how important the next person is. Never allow appreciation and gratitude to be extinct in your relationships. That's the glue that will help you to stay close to each other in the long run.

This chapter has shown us the importance of cultivating self-love to have a strong foundation for healthy and lasting relationships. Whatever you wish to have, envision it, and go for it. As long as you put in effort, the relationship will come alive. Be intentional all the way. There is no limit to how much depth and success you have when you wholeheartedly devote yourself to showing up as the best and most authentic version of yourself. It's only a matter of time before the landscape of your life starts to sprout with beautiful flowers of healthy and fulfilling relationships.

CHAPTER 6
FOSTERING LASTING HOLISTIC PERSONAL GROWTH

Change and growth take place when a person has risked himself and dares to become involved with experimenting with his own life.
-Herbert Otto

Achieving holistic success is one of the greatest ways to overcome the pain of a broken past or past failures. Filling your life with much to be grateful for is a great way to live an enriched and fulfilled life. In this chapter, we will be unpacking different ways you can grow in the various aspects of your life.

There will be days when you might glance back at your past and feel sad. However, if you fill your present life with the fruit of your toil and disciplined living, your present joy will supersede any past failures or disadvantages you faced. Let's explore the different strategies you can use to create a robust and successful life across every domain of your life. This way, your past doesn't have to hold you back anymore or be blamed for any current lack of progress or productivity you might be facing.

Being committed to personal development should be a lifelong promise you make to yourself. This is because there is so much potential locked up within us. One of the best gifts we can ever offer ourselves is to harness that potential, even though we might not always be confident to do so.

Pursuing holistic growth will help you to feel like you have achieved true healing inside out. It's one thing to feel great about ourselves, but it's another thing to wake up each day to a life we love. Therefore, your biggest responsibility is to create that life for yourself now. Write down whichever areas of your life you feel unhappy about and set clear goals of what you would like to achieve. It's time to take charge and invite more abundance into every angle of your life you can think about. Let's get started!

Financial Growth Strategies

Financial education is not just reserved for students who take on board that subject at formal institutions. It's a subject everyone has to learn since we live in a world where we rely on finances to look after our livelihoods. Below are key strategies you can use to develop a successful financial habit.

Diversifying Income Streams

Relying on one source of income can put a massive strain on you. It also brings with it lots of anxiety because there is always a level of uncertainty about the longevity of that income source. Think about different ways to grow your income base. It helps with financial security. For instance, you can use your savings to start a new business project, invest in a company by buying shares, or start an online e-commerce business.

Open a Savings Account and Pay Yourself First

Avoid overspending on unnecessary things by deciding on a practical percentage of your income you will save every month. Wouldn't it be good to pay yourself a lot? See it that way. You can save perhaps 40% of your income and keep it safe in your savings account. Doing this every month will put you on the route to achieving financial freedom.

Budget and Stick To What You Planned

It can be tempting to always slide into your savings account just because you know that it's your money. That habit leads to financial strain. Practice leaving below your means. Don't just buy something simply because you can. Plan how much you will spend, save, invest, and give to other courses or emergency things each  month. Respect your budget. You make a financial boundary to protect yourself from yourself and others draining up your finances unnecessarily.

Invest for Your Retirement Funds

Imagine being in your 60s or older and still having to wake up and work all day. How is that fair? Love yourself enough to give yourself a timeline for when you will put up with toiling. You can secure funds for your retirement funds starting as early as possible, even in your 20s. A hustle-free way to do so is to find a good investment plan and stick to it. If you invest your money, it allows you to gain profit over a long period. Imagine how much you would have raised by the time you are 60 years old if you started in your 20s. Even if you invested a small percentage of your income, it would still count over a long time, especially if you take an investment plan that involves compound interest.

Don't Take High-Interest Loans

A lot of loans are just a way to imprison yourself in financial debt. If you are unable to pay off things within five years, think twice before taking any big loan. If you need a loan, rather consider going for a lower-interest loan. Take your time to research; don't quickly accept any offer that first comes your way.

Pay Your Expenses on Time

When it comes to paying off things, avoid procrastinating. Paying bills on time helps you boost and keep your credit score good. When you have a higher credit score, you get more opportunities to get lower interest rates when you need to lend some money. You can use apps that will give you payment reminders to ensure that you will do everything on time.

Continue to Invest in Financial Education

There is so much you can learn about finances. Continue to read financial education newsletters and books about finances, and reach out to a financial advisor to learn new ways to make better financial decisions.

Look After Yourself

Yes, saving and spending less is important. However, it's also crucial to remember that you worked hard and deserve to treat yourself and celebrate your hard work. Each month, make it a ritual to do something special for yourself. Pamper yourself or get yourself something that you like. You might not feel like you need it, but it's still important to remind yourself that you are worthy of anything good in this life.

Achieving a Healthy Lifestyle

Living a healthy lifestyle will help you enjoy the quality of your life. Let's review some strategies to keep your body and mind in shape and also maintain a productive lifestyle.

Let Go of Ultra-Processed Meals and Sugar

Sadly, many highly palatable foods tend to be ultra-processed foods (UPFs). These are foods that have modified ingredients. Unfortunately, the things added are usually harmful to the body. Examples include frozen meals, processed cheese, and a lot of packaged cookies. Studies show that they often contain excess calories, which leads to obesity problems (Gunnars, 2023).

The same study also indicates how sugar-sweetened beverages can contribute to high blood pressure and type two diabetes. Examples include sodas, sweetened teas, and even fruit juices! You can opt for healthier options such as having spring water, unsweetened teas, and blending your juice from raw fruits.

Let go of eating too many refined carbs; rather find food with whole grains. Examples of refined carbs that can give you problems include things like added sugars, white flour, candy, pancakes, chocolates, and so on. Getting rid of refined carbs will also help you get rid of excess belly fat and reduce the production of stress cortisol.

Sleep Hygiene

Being awake between the hours of 11:00 p.m. and 4:00 a.m. can strain your brain and cause hormonal disruption. Have you ever felt sad for no reason when you stayed up late for hours? Chances are that it has a lot to do with your body being strained because it *needs* sleep to function well. You negatively affect your mental and physical performance when you deprive your body and mind of enough rest. Dim your lights or switch them off to help your body produce more melatonin (the sleep hormone) around the time you head to bed.

Take Care of Your Gut

Your body works hard day and night to keep you well cared for. Imagine how grateful it would be if you could only put more effort into supporting the hard work it already does. You can start by including in your diet-friendly bacteria that will promote optimal gut functions and prevent diseases. Examples include taking prebiotic supplements, eating yogurt, kimchi, feta cheese, and sauerkraut.

Majority of What Constitutes Your Meals Should Be Fruits and Vegetables. You probably heard it many times while growing up, but it's important to hear it again. Instead of making carbs a huge part of your meal, switch it up and make vegetables and fruits the main character. Your body needs more of those than carbs. They are packed with many minerals, antioxidants, vitamins, and more.

Avoid Substance Abuse

Drugs and alcohol only numb pain for a short while but keep you imprisoned for a painful life you won't like. Now that you have taken the path of holistic healing, it's time never to allow alcohol, cigarettes, or drugs to be a part of your life. If you don't have those addictions, think about any other unhealthy addictions you might be suffering from. For instance, binge eating, sex, gambling, and so on. Start practicing living a sober life you will be proud of. The more you face your wounds from the core, the easier it will be to live a free life because you won't have anything to hide or run away from anymore.

Become Friends With Spices and Herbs

Spices aren't just good for making your food taste great. They are also packed with lots of anti-inflammatory and multiple health benefits! Start applying as many species as possible because your meals will significantly boost your immunity.

Meditation and Journaling

Take time to look after your mental health by spending quality time with yourself. In the same way, it's important to do regular emotional check-in sessions with your loved one, the same way you should also do so with yourself. Journal how you feel. Think about different ways to problem-solve any concerns you may be having. Use your mirror to remind yourself how valuable and special you are.

Look directly at yourself and repeat positive affirmations until you sense no resistance to what those statements are planting in your soul. Avoid overthinking. It's better to brainstorm solutions during your meditation sessions than allow anxious thoughts to distract your peace throughout the day.

Achieving Social Success

Social success involves how well all your relationships are doing. This includes your family life, work friends, and other acquaintances you might have. Let's review some ways you can boost the quality of all your relationships. Most of the things about relationships were already covered in the previous chapters. However, in this section, we will explore more tips to get your social life soaring.

Research Places to Visit

Not sure what to do with your friends or where to go? The phone in your hand can solve your problems. All you have to do is research to find out more about events or cool locations to visit in your area or wherever you can afford to go. Make sure to pitch in on time so that you can have the entire time to socialize and make new friends. Take the initiative and make the first move to get to know someone.

Treat Yourself Well

People tend to be more attracted to someone who treats themselves well. Don't wait for others to make you feel good. Just show up for yourself more and prove that you already have your back. Change your closet from time to time. Don't compromise when it comes to self-care.

Talk to People You Don't Know

It feels a lot safer to just stick to someone we know whenever we go out. But that doesn't allow us to grow that much. When you visit social gatherings, mix and mingle. Don't just stay glued to someone you know. Allow yourself to feel awkward and make mistakes while attempting to make new friends; that's how you grow.

Join a Social Club

Having a group of friends whom you can deem as your support network in some way can help boost your mental health. Think about something you enjoy doing. For example, reading or dancing. Join a book or dance club where you can meet regularly and create lasting relationships.

Meet Up With Online Friends

You might have hundreds of thousands of Facebook or Instagram friends by now. Regardless of the number, try to build real-life relationships with people you notice can be a great match for you. You can challenge yourself to meet at least one or two new friends in real life every month. Keep an open mind; even if things don't go well on certain meet-ups, don't give up! Things will gradually fall into place if you keep trying. You soon meet people you can create unforgettable relationships with.

Plan to Meet Up With Old Friends

Another great idea is to resurrect your old relationships. They might be feeling stale or dry by now, but don't give up on them. Plan to stick to a specific date when you can meet up and bring a new lease of life into your connections.

Work on Your Active Listening Skills

When you feel nervous, it's usually because you are too focused on your insecurities and worried about what to say. Start to do the opposite. Instead of bringing the attention to yourself, actively focus on what others are saying. This will give you a better chance to hear what's being said and respond appropriately.

Give Genuine Compliments

People can usually sense flattery or a sense of compliment. Connect to people in authentic ways. Focus on what people do well. Compliment their true strengths. This will make them gravitate more towards you. When you give fake compliments, it breaks rapport and makes someone not trust your words anymore.

Spread Kindness

Whatever you give out tends to come right back at you. Start to show people more kindness and compassion. You are likely to be treated with the same level of courtesy most times.

Be More Approachable

When you walk into a room, don't you sometimes scan people's faces and body language to see who you can go to talk to? Some people's body language can make us uncomfortable talking to them, while others are good at being approachable.

You, too, can choose to become an approachable person by working on open body language and charismatic skills. You can smile more and make good eye contact. Hug and wave at people more. Instead of talking a lot about yourself, make the other person feel like the main character and allow them to talk about you. Treat other people kindly. When others watch you do that, it assures them that you will also give them the same treatment if they engage with you. Try not to be argumentative during discussions. When conflicts arise, try to de-escalate them by making others feel heard and respected.

Overcome Your Insecurities

People can sense how you feel about yourself and others. When your friends or family members detect that you are jealous of them, it can make them feel unsafe around you. Avoid having an unhealthy competitive spirit that makes people feel like you are always trying to be better than them. The only person you should be racing against is yourself. Focus on winning your race instead of trying to raise by dimming other people's light.

Invest in Yourself

Manage your expectations of their people. We often get disappointed when others don't meet our expectations and get bitter about it. However, it's important not to place this burden on others. Don't expect people to give you what you haven't learned to give yourself first. If there is something you deeply crave to have from others, look within and see if you have been depriving yourself of that thing. Work on finding ways to invest in your needs and dreams. Take responsibility for your happiness, and don't leave others to be responsible for it. When you always wait for people to look after you, you set yourself up for disappointment because the reality is that everyone is worried about their own lives. Work on having interdependent relationships instead of expecting too much from others.

Get What's Important Done First

You will feel less guilt about investing in your social activities if you first learn to manage your time effectively. Work on getting the five most important things done before mid-day. This will free your space up and also make you feel less stressed throughout the day. When you are less stressed, you will have better energy to put out in your relationships.

Forgive

You will err, and so will others too. Make it a happen to accept other people's attempts to repair broken relationships. If someone is

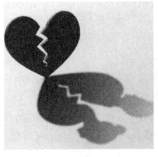

showing remorse and trying to make it up to you, don't punish them more and continue to be closed off. Practice telling people that you accepted their apology. Once you do share that you have forgiven someone, be careful of bringing up what they did when you have future conflicts. That will only prove that you didn't truly forgive them. It makes it hard for relationships to grow because you will always be judging people for the mistakes they made ages ago. Let go, and don't hoard people's errors anymore. It will also free your heart from carrying so much anger and resentment.

Support Your Friends and Family Members

Just handling your own life can be very busy and even overwhelming. However, that shouldn't be the reason why you fail to show up for others when they need you. Find ways to always serve your tribe. The more you sow in other people's lives, the more they, too, will be inspired to be concerned about your affairs. If there is any relationship you wish could grow, start to become the change you wish to see. Lead by example and be forthright about your intentions.

Find Ways to Make People Smile

You might be surprised to realize how very little encouragement people get even though it's something priceless we can always gift to others. Find ways to surprise people from time to time with unexpected gestures of love and goodwill. For instance, fix someone's makeup if you notice that they put it on the wrong way. Send a warm text to encourage your friends to study for exams or offer to help with cooking. Being more generous with your spirit will open people's hearts to loving you even more.

Challenge Yourself

You can do 30-day challenges to push yourself to become a greater version of who you can be. Each day can have at least one new thing you have to do to improve your social life. For example, have a difficult conversation with someone you don't get along with, or visit your grandmother's house and offer to give her a massage. Think about thoughtful ways to show your heart toward people. The only way people will see the goodness in your heart is if you dare to prove it through your actions. Mere words won't make a true difference. Always ask yourself how you can practically show up for others. Life has a beautiful way of mirroring back to us just how much effort we put in.

This chapter has shown us ways to boost the quality of your life and attract more success from every angle. Approach each day with a positive and grateful mind and see it as an opportunity for growth and enjoying the gift of life. Decide for yourself what each day is going to be like. Say out loud and declare exactly what you want to achieve before the end of each day. Setting specific, measurable, attainable, realistic, and time-bound goals will help you evaluate your success level. It will also help you stay motivated because nothing feels as good as seeing so much growth in your life.

CONCLUSION

Our inner child just wants us to acknowledge their pain. Your inner child is you. Don't let another day pass without giving your undivided attention and love to that part of you. Your lasting joy and happiness depend on how much work you will put in to free that child and prove that you care about their pain and dreams.

As we are nearing the end of this journey, it's time for you to think about the dreams you forgot along the way as you were chasing after survival. What did you use to dream of becoming as you were young? How did you envision your future? What were some interesting things you enjoyed doing in your childhood that you might have forgotten about as time elapsed?

If you were to relive your childhood days? What would you do right? Now, you can sit down like an architect and plan exactly what you want the rest of your life to be like. You may not have had much of a say in the life you got to live before, but guess who's in charge now? You are.

Take some time to write your vision and create a clear blueprint of who you will now choose to show up as. We become who we are meant to be by showing up as that person. That means that if your dream was to be a medical doctor, there's no use for you to go study accounting. If you love nature, why live in a city full of pollution and buildings only?

It's now time for you to connect to your authentic self and live a life that's true to the core of who you truly are. The fear might still exist, but don't let it stop you from moving forward. All it takes is bravery and a made-up mind to get things done. You have already made it all the way and finished reading this book. For that, I sincerely commend you. The time has now come to use all the knowledge you are equipped with to create the life of your dreams. Your inner child deserves to be given that gift.

Thank you for reading this book. I trust that it has been a wholesome and therapeutic journey for you. I look forward to reading your reviews on Amazon. May your journey ahead be full of countless success stories. Keep tapping into your greatness!

REFERENCES

Aletheia. (2019, April 6). *25 Signs you have a wounded inner child (and how to heal)*. LonerWolf. https://lonerwolf.com/feeling-safe-inner-child/

Cherry, K. (2022b, May 26). *The different types of attachment styles*. Verywell Mind. https://www.verywellmind.com/attachment-styles-2795344

Danielsson, M. (2022, September 23). *How to reach financial freedom: 12 habits to get you there*. Investopedia. https://www.investopedia.com/articles/personal-finance/112015/these-10-habits-will-help-you-reach-financial-freedom.asp

Grist, A. (2023, December 13). *Defining boundaries with inner child healing*. Amy Grist. https://amygrist.com/defining-boundaries-with-innerchild-healing/

Gunnars, K. (2019, June 7). *27 Health and nutrition tips that are actually evidence-based*. Healthline; Healthline Media. https://www.healthline.com/nutrition/27-health-and-nutrition-tips

Indeed Editorial team. (2022, November 30). *Career Development | Indeed.com Canada Self Development Quotes*. Indeed Career Guide. https://ca.indeed.com/career-advice/career-development/self-development%20quotes

Mandriota, M. (2021, October 14). *4 Types of attachment: What's your style?* Psych Central. https://psychcentral.com/health/4-attachment-styles-in-relationships

Merck, A. (2018, February 6). *4 Ways childhood trauma changes a child's brain and body.* Salud America. https://salud-america.org/4-ways-childhood-trauma-changes-childs-brain-body/

Miller, R. (2023, October 6). *Healing from childhood trauma: The process & effective therapy options.* Choosing Therapy. https://www.choosingtherapy.com/healing-from-childhood-trauma/

Moore, A. (2020, July 28). *Do you have an insecure attachment style? What it means + how to heal.* mbgmindfulness. https://www.mindbodygreen.com/articles/insecure-attachment-style

Ohanyan, V. (2021, April 22). *Build better boundaries with inner child work.* Womanly Inspiration. https://womanlyinspiration.com/articles/health/build-better-boundaries-with-inner-child

Perry, E. (2023, June 21). *Healthy relationships: 13 Valuable tips.* BetterUp. https://www.betterup.com/blog/healthy-relationships-in-life

Raypole, C. (2020, July 8). *8 Tips for healing your inner child.* Healthline.

https://www.healthline.com/health/mental-health/inner-child-healing

Raypole, C. (2021, February 5). *Habit Loop: What it is and how to break it.* Healthline. https://www.healthline.com/health/mental-health/habit-loop#takeaway

Stewart, A. R. (2017, November 17). *13 Habits of self-love every woman should adopt.* Healthline. https://www.healthline.com/health/13-self-love-habits-every-woman-needs-to-have#13.-Be-kind-to-yourself

Verity, S. (2022, November 14). *8 Tips for social success.* WebMD. https://www.webmd.com/balance/social-life-success

CLICK HERE

HEALING YOUR INNER CHILD

We sincerely hope you enjoyed our new book *"Healing Your Inner Child"*. We would greatly appreciate your feedback with an honest review at the place of purchase.

First and foremost, we are always looking to grow and improve as a team. It is reassuring to hear what works, as well as receive constructive feedback on what should improve. Second, starting out as an unknown author is exceedingly difficult, and Amazon reviews go a long way toward making the journey out of anonymity possible. Please take a few minutes to write an honest review.

Best regards,

Sofia Visconti

Printed by Amazon Italia Logistica S.r.l.
Torrazza Piemonte (TO), Italy

63790364R00111